Volume 4
SUMMER

ALL
together
NOW

for ages 4-12

13 Sunday school lessons
when you have kids
of all ages in one room

LOIS KEFFER
Author of ALL-IN-ONE SUNDAY SCHOOL

Group
Loveland, Colorado
group.com

Group resources really work!

This Group resource incorporates our R.E.A.L. approach to ministry. It reinforces a growing friendship with Jesus, encourages long-term learning, and results in life transformation, because it's

Relational
Learner-to-learner interaction enhances learning and builds Christian friendships.

Experiential
What learners experience through discussion and action sticks with them up to 9 times longer than what they simply hear or read.

Applicable
The aim of Christian education is to equip learners to be both hearers and doers of God's Word.

Learner-based
Learners understand and retain more when the learning process takes into consideration how they learn best.

All Together Now

Volume 4 — SUMMER

Copyright © 2013, Lois Keffer/0000 0000 3306 2815

• •

Visit our website: **group.com**

Unless otherwise indicated, all Scripture quotations are taken from the *Holy Bible*, New Living Translation, copyright © 1996, 2004, 2007. Used by permission of Tyndale House Publishers, Inc., Carol Stream, Illinois 60188. All rights reserved.

Credits
Author: Lois Keffer
Editors: Christine Yount Jones, Jennifer Hooks, Lee Sparks, and Deborah Helmers
Chief Creative Officer: Joani Schultz
Cover Designer: Jeff Spencer
Interior Designer: Jean Bruns
Production Artist: Suzi Jensen
Illustrator: Matt Wood

ISBN: 978-0-7644-8237-3
Printed in the United States of America.
15 14 13 12 11 10   25 24 23 22

Table of Contents

THE LESSONS

All Together Now

Introduction

Dear Friend in Children's Ministry,

Ah, summer—time for adventure! There's no better place to begin than *All Together Now, Volume 4*. This summer quarter is packed with Old Testament adventure from start to finish.

We kick off things with Joshua, a mighty man of God, and his strong and courageous leadership into the Promised Land. Having received the reins of leadership from Moses, Joshua stays true to the commands of the Lord God of Israel and leads the people to do the same. Wise in matters both military and spiritual, Joshua leads the army of Israel through the land of Canaan, conquering its kings and city-states and preparing the land for occupation by the 12 tribes of Israel.

For the young nation, as their obedience to God goes, so go their fortunes. When they become entangled in worship of the Canaanite god Baal, we find them destitute and preyed upon by bandits. It's Deborah, the wise judge, who forms a surprising coalition to defeat an oppressive Canaanite king and bring 40 years of peace to Israel.

The Israelites *demand* to have a king like other countries. The Lord relents and gives them Saul for a king. They cheer tall, handsome Saul, until he sins against God and madness overtakes him. Enter the extraordinary David. Chosen at a young age to be the next king, he spends years evading King Saul's jealous attacks, resisting opportunities to take revenge on Saul when the opportunity arises.

When he and his hungry men are refused food by a selfish rich man, David is about to take revenge when the lovely and wise Abigail stops him by offering food herself. Her selfish husband dies in a fit of anger and David takes Abigail as his own wife.

David's life shows the power of perseverance, of pursuing God even while evading those who would kill him. Throughout the hair-raising escapes and great victories of his life, David remains exemplary in his intimacy with God, penning psalms that still speak to our hearts today.

Generations of kings after David refused to remain faithful to the Lord. So the Lord calls the great prophet Elijah to challenge priests of the false god Baal to a fiery showdown on Mount Carmel. After Elijah's tremendous victory, Queen Jezebel's threats send him running and he learns how to hear God's still, small voice of encouragement.

We wrap up our summer adventures with the rule of a young boy king, Josiah, who finds the book of the Law and, with his devotion to God, turns his lost country on its ear. Young Josiah's reforms lead Israel back to her covenant relationship with the one true God. He leads his people in the first Passover celebration in many years. God once again blesses his people with his mighty presence—all because of what an 8-year-old boy started.

Your kids won't want to miss one week of this action-packed summer with Israel's heroes—men, women, and even kids. Prepare for young lives to be changed as you lead them in meeting the people whose courage and obedience formed the nation of Israel and set the stage for Jesus, the Messiah.

Lois Keffer

All Together Now

Active Learning in Combined Classes

Research shows people remember most of what they do but only a small percentage of what they hear—which means kids don't do their best learning just sitting around a table talking! They need to be involved in lively activities that help bring home the truth of the lesson. Active learning involves learning through experiences—experiences that help kids understand important principles, messages, and ideas.

Active learning is a discovery process that helps children internalize the truth as it unfolds. Kids don't sit and listen as a teacher tells them what to think and believe—they find out for themselves. Teachers also learn in the process!

Each active-learning experience in this book is followed by questions that encourage kids to share their feelings about what just happened. Further discussion questions help kids interpret their feelings and decide how this truth affects their lives. The final part of each lesson challenges kids to decide what they'll do with what they've learned—how they'll apply it to their lives during the coming week.

How do kids feel about active learning? They love it! Sunday school becomes exciting, slightly unpredictable, and more relevant and life-changing than ever before. So move the table aside, gather your props, and prepare for some unique and memorable learning experiences!

Active learning works beautifully in combined classes. Whether the group is playing a game or acting out a Bible story, kids of all ages can participate on an equal level. You don't need to worry about reading levels and writing skills. Everyone gets a chance to make important contributions to class activities and discussions.

These simple classroom tips will help you get your combined class off to a smooth start:

☐ When kids form groups, aim for an equal balance of older and younger kids in each group. Encourage the older kids to act as coaches to help younger ones get in the swing of each activity.

☐ In "pair-share," everyone works with a partner. When it's time to report to the whole group, each person tells his or her partner's response. This simple technique teaches kids to listen and to cooperate with each other.

☐ If an activity calls for reading or writing, pair young nonreaders with older kids who can lend their skills. Older kids enjoy the esteem-boost that comes with acting as a mentor, and younger kids appreciate getting special attention and broadening their skills.

☐ Don't worry too much about discussion going over the heads of younger children. They'll be stimulated by what they hear the older kids saying. You may be surprised to find some of the most insightful discussion literally coming "out of the mouths of babes."

☐ Make it a point to give everyone—not just those who are academically or athletically gifted—a chance to shine. Affirm kids for their cooperative attitudes when you see them working well together and encouraging each other.

☐ Keep in mind kids may give unexpected answers. That's OK. When kids give "wrong" answers, don't correct them. Say something like: "That's interesting. Let's look at it from another viewpoint." Then ask for ideas from other kids. If you correct their answers, most kids will soon stop offering them.

How to Get Started With All Together Now

TEACHING STAFF

When you combine Sunday school classes, teachers get a break! Teachers who would normally be teaching in your 4- to 12-year-old age groups may want to take turns. Or ask teachers to sign up for the Sundays they'll be available to teach.

LESSONS

The lessons in the *All Together Now* series are grouped by quarter—fall, winter, spring, and summer—but each lesson can also stand on its own.

PREPARATION

Each week you'll need to gather the easy-to-find supplies in the You'll Need section and photocopy the reproducible handouts. Add to that a careful read of the lesson and Scripture passages, and you're ready to go!

Quick-Grab Activities—Plan in a Can

By Cynthia Crane and Sharon Stratmoen
Reprinted by permission of Children's Ministry Magazine. © Group Publishing, Inc. All rights reserved.

It's Sunday morning and you've just finished your entire lesson. You check the clock, and although the service should be ending, you hear no music, see no parents coming down the hall. What you *do* hear is your senior pastor, still excited about the message. And then you quickly begin trying to figure out what you're going to do with a room full of kids and no lesson left.

You need a survival kit. A bucket of backup, a plan in a can. So we've created two kits you can build on your own and store in your room. When you have extra time with kids, don't sweat it—just pull out your plan in a can and get busy!

In case you're wondering, Why call it a can? Why not a box or a bin or a bucket? For those times when you're worrying whether you'll be able to keep kids' attention and bust their boredom, the name is a sweet reminder that yes, you can!

PLAN IN A CAN: Games Galore!

. . . .

THE INGREDIENTS

☐ Faithful Faces cards (printed photos, poster board, adhesive, and a laminator or clear adhesive vinyl) held together with a rubber band

☐ sidewalk chalk

☐ Christian music CDs for kids

☐ black-light lamp

☐ 2 large happy-face images

☐ 2 colors of plastic clothespins (enough for 3 per child; available at dollar stores)

FAITHFUL FACES ▸▸ Kids love the Memory Game, where shuffled cards are laid out facedown in a grid and kids try to find matching cards by turning over two at a time. (If they don't get a match, they turn the cards back facedown and the next person goes. If they do get a match, they get another turn.) So why not capitalize on this fun game to model and reinforce the important faithful faces in kids' lives? Just take pictures of the kids in your class, missionaries in your church, Bible friends you've been learning about, families you're praying for, and people in your congregation. Then whip up your own version of the game.

Use photo paper or regular printer paper to print out two of each photo, and mount them on poster board. Run the poster board through a laminator or apply clear adhesive vinyl, and you've got a game worth talking about. Kids will love finding their friends. And when they get a match, throw in a little challenge by giving them an extra point if they can remember names and other details about the person on the card.

SIDEWALK CHALK OF TODAY'S TALK ▸▸ Form groups of two to six, and hand out sidewalk chalk. You can have as many or as few groups as you have sidewalks for. Have groups work together to draw one picture on concrete that says something about the day's Bible story. When parents pick up their kids, you get a huge blessing: The kids tell their parents what they learned without being prompted. As a bonus, take photos of kids and their drawings for a quick recap to start off the following week's lesson. You can even make a month-in-review bulletin board starring your kids as the teachers.

MUSIC FREEZE ▸▸ If you think an hour is a long time for you, it's like dog years to kids. They have wiggles they've got to get out. So when you have extra time, turn up the music and let kids be as goofy as they want—until the music stops. Then they have to freeze in place. Give this a twist by adding a black light. Changing your environment is a great break from the everyday, and it lets kids know that you always have a few surprises in store.

CLOTHESPIN TAG ▸▸ You can use this game to remind kids that no thief can steal our joy when we go to the Joy Source: God. Place the happy-face images on the floor at opposite ends of a play area. Form two teams, and have each team go to one happy face. Assign each team a color of clothespin. Pin three clothespins to the back of each child's clothing above the waist. The goal of the game is for each team to try to steal the other team's clothespins and drop them on their own team's happy face. Play music to signal "go." Let kids play for one minute or so, and then turn off the music to signal "stop." After a few starts and stops, end the game, declare the team with the most clothespins as the winner, and then let kids get more "joy" on their backs and play again. When you're done, remind kids that they can always find new joy with God.

PLAN IN A CAN: Craft Creations
....

THE INGREDIENTS

- ☐ Legos in a resealable bag
- ☐ Moon Sand sculpting sand
- ☐ PlayFoam sculpting material
- ☐ window crayons
- ☐ Window Writers
- ☐ whiteboard markers
- ☐ Magic Nuudles cornstarch building blocks
- ☐ giant chenille pipe cleaners
- ☐ Bendaroos sculpting sticks
- ☐ one-subject notebook
- ☐ colored pencils
- ☐ Glitter Putty
- ☐ construction paper
- ☐ washable markers
- ☐ SuperBalls
- ☐ Christian music CDs for kids

CREATE ▶▶ If you have time to burn as kids are arriving, try this activity. Have kids use Legos building blocks, Moon Sand sculpting sand, PlayFoam sculpting material, Window Writers, or whiteboard markers to create a symbol of something that happened during the week. Then have kids show their creations as they say: "Hi, my name is _____, and I created this _____, because last week _____."

RESPOND ▶▶ Let kids use any craft supplies from the can to create a symbol of what the day's lesson meant to them. For instance, kids can draw a picture or write how they'll apply the point to life, using the windows, a whiteboard, or paper. Or they might choose to create a symbol that reminds them of what they learned, using giant chenille pipe cleaners or Bendaroos sculpting sticks. Invite kids to share what their creations represent.

PRAY ▶▶ Create a class prayer journal with a notebook for kids to write prayer notes in. Have kids all write their names on the cover because the journal belongs to all of them. Take out the journal throughout the year. Encourage kids to take turns writing their prayers or notes using colored pencils. If kids are stumped, give them prayer prompts such as "I thank God for…" "I need help with…" and "I pray for…" Close your time with prayer, and include requests from the prayer journal.

CHILL ▶▶ Give kids Glitter Putty, SuperBalls, or simply space. Play Christian music and let kids just "chill" as they quietly listen. Use the following tactile treats to help them focus on the music. As they listen, let them squish Glitter Putty between their fingers, play with SuperBalls, or simply relax on the floor at least 5 feet away from anyone else and close their eyes.

All Together Now

Be Strong and Courageous

LESSON AIM

To help kids know that ★ *with God's help we can be strong and courageous.*

OBJECTIVES

Kids will

✓ tell about a courageous moment,

✓ run a "background check" as they're introduced to Joshua,

✓ make a "Pocketful of Courage" to carry with them, and

✓ talk about when they might need to be strong and courageous this week.

BIBLE BASIS

 **Deuteronomy 31:1-8; 34:1-9; Joshua 1:1-9**

Here's a job description for you: Follow in the shoes of Moses and lead the multitudes of homeless Israelites. Oh, and while you're at it, conquer the Promised Land and its many fortified city-states. God had just the leader primed and ready for the task: Moses' long-time assistant, Joshua, son of Nun. In Hebrew, his name is pronounced *Yehoshua*, meaning, *Yahweh is salvation*.

Joshua had been at Moses' side since the Exodus. In the battle against the Amalekites (Exodus 17) he proved to be a strong military leader. He was one of the original 12 spies Moses sent into the Promised Land, and one of only two who had the faith

You'll need...

☐ a copy of "The Joshua Files" handout (pp. 16-17)

☐ scissors

☐ paper

☐ markers

☐ pencils

☐ Bibles in an easy-to-read translation

☐ copies of the "Pocketful of Courage" handout (p. 20)

to urge the nation to go in and take the land and possess it (Numbers 14:6-9). He was Moses' right-hand man when God delivered the Ten Commandments, allowed to accompany Moses part of the way up the holy mountain (Exodus 32:17).

As soon as we start the book of Joshua, we see that Joshua's leadership would be different from that of Moses, who mainly stood as intercessor between God and the people. Joshua took on the roles of both spiritual leader and military commander. And, as he had been clearly taught by Moses, he believed that military success would come only as the nation continued in loyalty and faithfulness to the God of Israel.

Joshua's task required a person of great wisdom and great might. He had to take the generation of Hebrews who'd been born during the desert wanderings, make an army of them, and then go into Canaan and conquer its long-established city-states. Meanwhile, he had to keep the people well-provisioned, following God, and at peace with one another. Finally it would fall to Joshua to mete out the newly conquered land to Israel's 12 tribes.

So, as Joshua started out, God challenged him to be strong and courageous. Before dying, Moses gave this same charge when he dedicated Joshua as the next leader. God repeated this charge over and over. Finally, even the people charged Joshua to be strong and courageous (Joshua 1:18). As a result, Joshua never failed as a leader.

Ephesians 6:10-11

This passage is the introduction to Paul's famous "Armor of God" passage. What an interesting Old Testament/New Testament contrast! While God was preparing Joshua to go to war, Paul encouraged the church at Ephesus to suit up to fight the plans of Satan. God was preparing Joshua for physical conquest under the old covenant; Paul was preparing Christians for spiritual warfare under the new. Both circumstances require courage, determination, obedience, and heavy reliance on God's help.

UNDERSTANDING YOUR KIDS

If you had it to do over, would you want to go through childhood again? I certainly wouldn't.

Think back to the joys and challenges of *your* childhood. What warm, happy memories come to mind? What moments would you not want to revisit for anything in the world?

All Together Now

Kids need to be strong and courageous to face those first days in a new school, first contact with cliques, social gaffes that make them wish the floor would open up and swallow them, and times when there isn't a good friend to be found, a teacher just doesn't understand, or there's a bully on the loose. The potholes in kids' lives are deep and painful. Kids grow and mature by simply stepping in a few, falling, picking themselves up, and going on. They learn that tomorrow's a new day and even the worst moments are survivable. But—most important of all—★ *with God's help we can be strong and courageous* because we have a God who'll never leave or forsake us.

Use this lesson to inspire kids to place their confidence daily in the loving God who is all around them. Let them know that no matter what challenges life presents, they, like Joshua, can be strong and courageous because of God's presence.

THE LESSON »

ATTENTION GRABBER
· ·
Courage All Around

Greet kids warmly as they arrive and have them gather in a discussion circle.

Say: **We spend a lot of our time here exploring the amazing things God does—and we'll do that this morning. But first, think for a moment about a time *you* showed amazing courage. Maybe you helped keep a younger brother or sister calm during a big, scary storm. Or perhaps you stood up to kids who were picking on someone.**

To give you time to think about your courageous moment, I'll tell you about one of mine.

Briefly share a time when God helped you be courageous in a difficult situation. Temper your story so it's not too scary for the younger ones in your group.

Then allow kids around the circle to share their courageous moments. Make sure even the quietest kid has a chance to share such a moment.

Thank kids for sharing their stories.

Ask:

• **What helped you be strong and courageous when you had to be?**

Say: **Today we're going to learn that ★ *with God's help we can be strong and courageous.* You'll meet a Bible person right at the beginning of the great career God had planned for him. But first you'll check his background from the information the Bible gives us. Often before people are hired for a job, they have to go through a background check. Employers look at the records of people applying for jobs to see if they've ever broken the law, how they've done at paying their bills, if they've been good employees at other jobs, and so on.**

We're going to do our own background check on this Bible person. Are you ready to take it on? Let's do it!

All Together Now

BIBLE EXPLORATION

The Joshua Files (Deuteronomy 31:1-8; 34:1-9; Joshua 1:1-9)

Say: **As today's story begins, the people of Israel are about to get a new leader. They've had just one leader for over 40 years: Moses. He stood up to Pharaoh and brought the Israelites out of slavery in the land of Egypt.**

Moses led the Israelites through the desert for 40 years. Finally they moved toward the Promised Land on the far side of the Jordan River and conquered all the lands there. Moses knew he would never enter the Promised Land himself, but before Moses died, God told him to prepare Israel's next great leader. And who could possibly take Moses' place? God had just the perfect person in mind.

In a moment I'll have you form groups. Each group will get one part of the Joshua files. Read through the information you have together, and then decide how you'll present it to the rest of us. For instance, you might want to do a drawing or a quick set of drawings, a news report, a skit or even a cartoon. You'll have just a few minutes, so be quick!

Have kids form four groups (one person can be a group). Give each group one of the Joshua Files and paper, markers, and pencils. Circulate among groups as they work to answer questions and make sure they get started in a good direction. Give a two-minute warning so kids can wrap up their work and clean their area; then have groups do their Joshua Files presentations in order. Fill in any quick details you feel the kids may have missed, and have kids give a rousing round of applause to each group.

Prep Box

Make a copy of "The Joshua Files" (pp. 16-17). Cut apart the four sections of the handout.

2. Joshua Goes With Moses Up Mount Sinai

Then the Lord said to Moses, "Come up to me on the mountain. Stay there, and I will give you the tablets of stone on which I have inscribed the instructions and commands so you can teach the people." So Moses and his assistant Joshua set out, and Moses climbed up the mountain of God.

Exodus 24:12-13

THE JOSHUA FILES

Historical Note: When Moses went up to the mountain of God to receive the Ten Commandments, no others but Joshua and some Israelite elders were allowed to come close to the mountain or they would die. And only Joshua went part way up the mountain with Moses. How will you present this part of Joshua's story to the entire group?

---

1. Joshua Is a Brave Warrior

While the people of Israel were still at Rephidim, the warriors of Amalek attacked them. Moses commanded Joshua, "Choose some men to go out and fight the army of Amalek for us. Tomorrow, I will stand at the top of the hill, holding the staff of God in my hand." So Joshua did what Moses had commanded and fought the army of Amalek... As a result, Joshua overwhelmed the army of Amalek in battle.

Exodus 17:8-10, 13

THE JOSHUA FILES

Historical Note: When the Israelites left Egypt, a band of roving bandits attacked their long train of people. Moses made Joshua captain of the men who went to drive away the Amalekites. With God's help, Joshua won a huge victory! How will you present this part of Joshua's story to the entire group?

3. Joshua and Caleb Are the Only Two Faithful Spies

Two of the men who had explored the land, Joshua son of Nun and Caleb son of Jephunneh, tore their clothing. They said to all the people of Israel, "The land we traveled through and explored is a wonderful land! And if the Lord is pleased with us, he will bring us safely into that land and give it to us. It is a rich land flowing with milk and honey. Do not rebel against the Lord, and don't be afraid of the people of the land. They are only helpless prey to us! They have no protection, but the Lord is with us! Don't be afraid of them!"

Numbers 14:6-9

THE JOSHUA FILES

Historical Note: When thousands of Israelites finally crossed the desert and made it to the Promised Land, Moses sent 12 spies to scout the land. Ten spies reported, "Oh, no—the people of that land are giants! We can never conquer them!" Only two spies, Joshua and Caleb, urged the people to trust God and not be afraid. How will you present this part of Joshua's story to the entire group?

---

4. Moses Dedicates Joshua; The Israelites Follow Joshua

Then Moses called for Joshua, and as all Israel watched, he said to him, "Be strong and courageous! For you will lead these people into the land that the Lord swore to their ancestors he would give them. You are the one who will divide it among them as their grants of land. Do not be afraid or discouraged, for the Lord will personally go ahead of you. He will be with you; he will neither fail you nor abandon you."

Deuteronomy 31:7-8

Now Joshua son of Nun was full of the spirit of wisdom, for Moses had laid his hands on him. So the people of Israel obeyed him, doing just as the Lord had commanded Moses.

Deuteronomy 34:9

THE JOSHUA FILES

Historical Note: Joshua had been Moses' assistant since he was a young man. Before Moses died, God told him to dedicate Joshua as the new leader of Israel in front of all the people. This was a huge job for Joshua! How will you present this part of Joshua's story to the entire group?

Ask:

• **Tell what you think of Joshua so far.**

• **Why might he be a good choice for Israel's leader?**

Say: **You might be interested in Joshua's job description as he takes over as Israel's leader. It goes something like this. First, make sure everyone in a camp of thousands of people has plenty to eat and drink and that they all get along.**

Ask:

• **Which one of you would like that job? Stand up.**

Encourage a child volunteer to stand.

Say: **Second, train a strong army of mighty men.**

Ask:

• **Who would stand up to take that job?**

Encourage a child volunteer to stand.

Say: **Great, thank you.**

Third, conquer a whole land full of people who have been there for thousands of years.

Ask:

• **Do I have a volunteer for that job?**

Encourage a child volunteer to stand up. Say: **Super! Now, can you even think about one person doing all these things at once? That's why God had a super-important message for Joshua as he began his new job. Let's read it together.** Have your child volunteers sit.

Here's how it works. Every time you hear the words *be strong and courageous* **or** *be strong and very courageous,* **pump your fist in the air three times and say** *Hoo! Hoo! Hoo!*

Have kids practice that response, then have willing readers take turns reading Joshua 1:1-9 and then 16-17 aloud.

Ask:

• **Take a great big guess here: What do you think God wanted Joshua to be?**

Say: **You got it! And this should be no surprise:** ★ *With God's help we can be strong and courageous,* **too!**

Ask:

• **What was the coolest thing you learned about Joshua that you can use in your life this week?**

All Together Now

LIFE APPLICATION

Staying Strong

Say: **You may not have noticed, but God not only told Joshua to be strong and courageous, he also told Joshua** *how* **to be strong and courageous.** ★ *With God's help we can be strong and courageous,* **too, so let's pay attention to the** *how* **part.**

Have kids open their Bibles to Joshua 1. Ask a volunteer child to read verses 7 and 8 aloud.

Ask:

• **How can we follow the patterns God set for Joshua?**

• **How does spending time with God make us more strong and courageous?**

• **What are other good ways to spend time with God?**

Say: **Reading the Bible and praying remind us that God is all-powerful, that he's with us, and that he loves us. When you face a situation that calls for courage, those are super-important things to remember.**

COMMITMENT

Pocketful of Courage

Say: **Wouldn't it be great if you could just carry a pocketful of courage with you wherever you went? Well, I've got some good news for you: You can!**

Give kids the "Pocketful of Courage" handouts. Instructions for cutting and folding the handouts are printed on the handouts. Older kids can help younger ones if they need it. When they're finished, the handouts fold into neat little pockets containing Joshua 1:9 that kids can carry wherever they go.

Ask:

• **When do you realize that God is with you?**

• **How does it make you feel to know that God is with you wherever you go?**

Say: ★ *With God's help we can be strong and courageous.* **When you need a reminder of that, hang on to your little Pocketful of Courage and read God's message to Joshua—and to you!**

Pocketful of Courage

Joshua could be strong and courageous because God promised to be with him wherever he went. God will be with everyone who loves him and serves him!

Cut out this clever little folding reminder of God's presence and care for you, and keep a pocketful of courage wherever you go!

1. Cut out the cross.

2. Cut the solid slits.

3. With the blank side facing up, fold in on the dark dotted lines, first the square with text beginning "For the Lord," next the other square with text, and finally the squares with the slits.

4. Tuck the slits together.

Your Pocketful of Courage is ready to go!

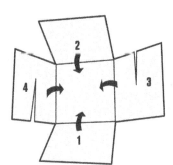

THIS IS MY COMMAND —
BE STRONG AND COURAGEOUS!
DO NOT BE AFRAID OR
DISCOURAGED.

POCKETFUL OF
COURAGE

JOSHUA 1:9

FOR
THE LORD YOUR GOD
IS WITH YOU WHEREVER
YOU GO.

Ask:

• **When do you think you might need a reminder to be strong and courageous this week?**

• **What part of this verse encourages you the most?**

CLOSING

. . . .

Face-to-Face Challenge

Have the kids form two lines facing each other. Have Line 1 say, "Be strong!" Then have Line 2 answer, "And courageous!"

Start with a whisper, and then have kids increase the volume gradually until they're shouting their lines. Then stop both sides and complete the closing by saying:

For the Lord your God is with you wherever you go!

Dismiss kids warmly and encourage them to come back to the next lesson.

Rahab the Brave

LESSON AIM

To help kids know that ★ *anyone can come to God in faith.*

OBJECTIVES

Kids will

✓ spy on various activities in the church,

✓ learn how Rahab from Jericho helped the Israelite spies,

✓ make a "Rahab's Window" craft, and

✓ ask God to help them see people through his eyes.

BIBLE BASIS

 **Joshua 2:1-23**

Joshua planned his attack point to gain entry into the Promised Land to be right in the middle of the fertile region that surrounded the Jordan River. By attacking in the middle, the kings from the north and south couldn't form an alliance to help each other.

The gem of this region was the city of Jericho, sometimes called the City of Palms. To this day Jericho is a resort area in the winter, noted for its lush green landscape fed by the Jordan River in an otherwise dry and thirsty land. It was an old city in the time of Joshua, with inner and outer walls dating from the Bronze Age. And in New Testament times, Jesus visited Jericho, which was the setting for the famous encounter with Zacchaeus in Luke's Gospel.

These formidable walls were wide enough to accommodate houses being built into them, and so it was with Rahab's house.

You'll need...

☐ copies of the "Rahab's Window" handout (p. 31)

☐ scissors

☐ 5 inches of scarlet yarn, ribbon, or other trim per child

☐ tape

Interestingly, there is some scholarly discussion about whether Rahab was truly a prostitute or merely an innkeeper. Since innkeepers were commonly both, it's possible that she was just given the name that commonly went with her position. Josephus, the ancient Jewish historian, referred to her simply as an innkeeper. The dispute about Rahab's true occupation is carried forward even today, with strong opinions on both sides. One interesting factor in the discussion is that she was drying flax on her roof. Flax was used to make clothing, implying that Rahab might have been both an innkeeper and a maker of fine clothing.

An interesting split in Christian and Jewish thinking is that the Jews believe Rahab eventually married Joshua himself, while Christians believe she married another Jew named Salmon and became the mother of Boaz, who in turn married Ruth. Rahab is prominently listed in the ancestry of Jesus (Matthew 1:5), indicating that God welcomes believers of all backgrounds. She's also listed as an example of faith in Hebrews 11:31.

And Jewish historians recognize Rahab as one of the greatest heroines of the Old Testament and *the* greatest convert to Judaism. They portray her to be honored by God as an ancestress of the prophet Ezekiel and the priestess Huldah.

Rahab was not only eager to help the two spies Joshua sent, but she also professed her faith in the living God. Over 40 years after the event, she was well acquainted with the account of God parting the Red Sea for the Israelites to cross. There was no doubt in her mind that the God of Israel ruled over the affairs of men. Without a thought she risked her life by lying to the king of Jericho about the Israelite spies' whereabouts and then helped the spies in a daring escape, asking only for her life and the lives of her family in return when the Israelite army came to destroy the city. The sign to keep her family safe? A scarlet cord hung from the window—more than a little reminiscent of the red marks painted on the doors of the Israelites at the first Passover to keep the death angel from visiting their homes.

And so an unlikely woman of faith played an unlikely role in setting up Israel's eventual victory over the formidable walled city of Jericho—then she became part of the lineage of Jesus himself. There goes God, operating outside the box again!

Throughout the story text, we'll refer to Rahab as an innkeeper to keep our lesson kid-friendly. The key point is, after all, no matter what her profession, she was a woman whose faith lay totally and securely in the Lord God of Israel.

All Together Now

📖 Galatians 3:26-29

Strictly speaking, Jewish law would have condemned Rahab. And if she were indeed a prostitute, she'd have been considered the lowest of the low. Being a foreigner made her subject to slaughter along with the rest of the idol-worshipping population of Jericho.

But the Spirit of God sent the Israelite spies to just the right woman—one who was already in awe of the great God of Israel. Don't you love it when God does things like that!

I have to share a personal experience here. A small church we once served decided to share the gospel outside a mystic fair. We met folks with a ready smile, a simple pamphlet about Jesus being Lord over both the seen and unseen, and a little sheet of information about our church. We mostly worked in twos, but I was alone on this duty when two big, bad bikers showed up, parked their roaring machines near me, and dismounted, their well-muscled arms bristling with tattoos. They looked around and then headed straight for me. I did my best shrinking-into-the-shrubbery act, only to be caught by one monster arm. The biker attached to the arm pulled me into a hug, and said, "God bless you for being here. These folks are so lost and really need this message." Utterly dumbfounded, I practiced deep breathing for the next couple of minutes to regain my composure, while readjusting my concept about the people God relies on to advance his kingdom.

Rahabs, bikers—God sends his message in all kinds of clay pots. If we allow God to open our eyes to them, we'll find brothers and sisters in our faith who'll help the kingdom in ways we can't begin to measure.

UNDERSTANDING YOUR KIDS

It's easy for kids to get the idea that all people who follow Jesus should look and sound like the people they're around at church. Early, varied faith-based experiences can help dispel that mistaken assumption. Though your kids are young, they can help sort and pack at events such as local food pantries and other in-town mission trips. It's important for kids to gain a broad perspective of what God's kingdom in the world looks like.

Use this lesson to encourage kids to look outside their church walls for people who are serving God in unique ways.

THE LESSON »

ATTENTION GRABBER

Spies on a Mission!

Greet kids warmly and tell them you have something extra special in store.

Say: **This morning we're going learn about three super-brave people: two Israelite spies and an innkeeper who helped them. I thought a good way to get ready for our Bible story would be to go on a spying mission of our own!**

Here's the plan: We're going to tiptoe around the church and spy on the good things that are happening. Remember— as spies, we don't want to be seen or heard. Our job is to check out what's going on without getting caught!

Lead your kids in a quick, stealthy look at the various activities happening around your church at the same time as your class. Let kids have a quick listen at the door of an adult class, a peek into the nursery, or a sneak look at what teenagers are doing. If you wish, you might beckon to a friendly "informant" from another room who will tiptoe out and give your group of spies special information about what's going on there. If there are treats to be had somewhere in the church, be sure you spy on that room. Then lead your spies tiptoeing back to your own room.

Ask:

• **Describe what cool things you discovered.**

• **Suppose you had a real spy job. What might that be like?**

• **Suppose someone said, "I'm a spy, and I need your help." What would you do?**

Say: **The spies in our Bible passage had an honest-to-goodness spy job—and if they hadn't gotten help from a friendly innkeeper, they might have gotten caught! During their spying adventure, I think they were surprised to find out that ★** *anyone can come to God in faith.* **Let's find out what happened.**

Teacher Tip

One teacher can easily take groups of about six "spies." If you have more than six children in your group, you may want to consider forming two groups and having an adult assistant take the second group.

BIBLE EXPLORATION

Rahab and the Spy Guys (Joshua 2:1-23)

Say: **Joshua and the Israelites were camped just across the Jordan River from the city of Jericho. Even back in Bible**

All Together Now

times, Jericho was an ancient city. It had two tall city walls, one inside the other. Now, the Israelites knew they had to solve a pretty tough problem: How could an army attack a city with not one, but two tall city walls?

Joshua, the commander of the Lord's armies, was a smart leader. Before he made any plans, he wanted to find out as much as he could about what the city was like on the inside and what the people of the city were thinking. So he chose two men to be spies. He had them dress up to look like people of Jericho. That's a pretty smart plan. Now let's have some of you help tell the rest of the story.

Choose two child volunteers to be the spies, one to be Rahab the innkeeper, one to be the king, and one or two to be messengers. Have two or more children serve as the city gates and wall.

Say: **Let's place the king on a chair far back in the city. Messengers, you sit on the floor by the king. City gates and wall, come forward. Rahab, your house is on the city wall, so you stand near the gates. Great—now everything is set. Listen carefully for your part as the story goes on. Act out exactly what the story tells you to do, OK? On with the story!**

When the *city gates opened, the spies walked right in.* Since they were dressed like everyone else, no one thought they were suspicious. *The spies* knew they should find a place to stay, so they *went to the inn that was built right into the city wall. There they met Rahab, the innkeeper. Then the spies walked around the city.* They looked at how it was built. They listened to what the people had to say. Then they *hurried back to the inn* and talked about what they would tell Joshua, the leader of their army.

In the meantime, *messengers told the king* that strangers had been seen in the city. The king and the messengers knew that the huge nation of Israelites was camped just across the Jordan River. They also knew that the Israelites had conquered people wherever they went. *The king got scared and started to shake!* How soon would the great armies of Israel attack his city? Would the city walls be able to hold them out? What should he do?

The messengers and the king talked together. What if those strangers were Israelite spies? Oh, no! If they were, they had seen the inside the city! They knew just how the city walls were built! They knew that all the people of Jericho were afraid of them!

I've got to take swift action, *the king thought.* Strangers often stayed at Rahab's inn on the city wall. What if the strangers were staying there? Maybe the messengers could catch them! *Go! Go! the king told the messengers. Check Rahab's inn! See if those spies are hiding there!*

While the king was still thinking, *Rahab was finding a good hiding place for the spies. She took them up to her flat roof* where she had bundles of flax lying in the sun to dry. *Rahab had the spies lie down, and she covered them with the bundles of flax so they were completely hidden.* Smart Rahab! No one would think to look for the spies on her roof under bundles of flax—she hoped. If she were caught hiding the spies, it would mean death for all of them.

As soon as the spies were safely hidden, *Rahab went downstairs and began cooking the evening meal* as she did every day, to make it look like everything was normal.

As the sun went down, *the city gates closed.*

Sure enough, *the king's messengers came rushing to Rahab's inn. They asked her about the two strangers. She told them,* "Oh, they were here, but they left just before the city gates closed. If you hurry, maybe you can catch them!"

So the king's messengers ordered the city gates to open and went rushing out of town to find the spies.

Meanwhile, Rahab went back up to the roof to talk to the two spies.

"I know that the Lord has given you this land," she told them. "Everyone here is scared to death of your people. We remember all the great things God has done for you. Why, he even dried up the Red Sea so you could escape from Egypt! The Lord your God is the true God in heaven above and on earth below!"

The two spies were surprised. They could see that Rahab believed in the one true God.

Rahab went on. "Promise me that you'll show kindness to me and my family because I've shown kindness to you today. Give me a sign that when you come in to conquer the city, you'll let me and my family live."

The spies agreed. "Our lives for your lives," they said. "Hang this red rope from your window and gather everyone from your family here in this house. When our armies attack, everyone in this house will be saved."

So Rahab tied the red rope from her window. Then she helped the spies escape down the city wall through her window.

All Together Now

The spies got away into the hills and hid for three days. Though the king's messengers looked, they could never find the spies.

Finally the spies sneaked across the Jordan River and reported everything to Joshua.

Great job, everyone! That was fine acting. Now please join me here in a circle. Have kids join you in a discussion circle.

Ask:

• **What report do you think the spies gave to their leader Joshua?**

• **Describe what surprised you about Rahab.**

• **Why do you think Rahab was willing to be such a good helper to the spies?**

Say: **It's pretty amazing that Rahab knew about the God of the Israelites. The Israelites had never been to Jericho, but Rahab had heard how God helped them cross the Red Sea more than 40 years before! Not only that, but Rahab believed in the one true God, just from the little bit she knew.**

Suppose Rahab had been caught hiding the spies. She would have been in one heap of trouble. But from just the little bit she knew about God, she trusted him to take care of her and her family. Rahab's story shows us that ★ *anyone can come to God in faith.*

Ask:

• **How do you think Rahab could be a traitor to her people in Jericho but also a follower of God?**

• **Think of someone at school or in your neighborhood who you consider unfriendly or really unlike you. Explain whether you think that person could also believe in God.**

Say: **We never know where we'll meet people who believe in God. Like these spies in Jericho, if we learn to look at people through God's eyes, we'll meet other people in the most surprising places who believe in God!**

LIFE APPLICATION
. . . .
Rahab's Window

Say: **We don't know the names of the spies who crept into the city of Jericho to check it out. But we *do* know the name of the woman in Jericho who helped them. It was—say it with me all together now—*Rahab!***

Prep Box

Make a sample "Rahab's Window" craft for kids to see. Set out copies of "Rahab's Window" (p. 31); scissors; tape; and 5-inch lengths of scarlet yarn, ribbon, or other trim on a craft table.

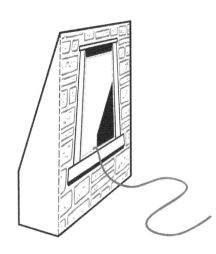

What's *really* strange about that is that God's orders were to wipe out the people of Jericho. Those people worshipped idols—not God—and God didn't want the Israelites to learn any of their unfaithful ways. But there was Rahab, ready to put her life on the line to help the Israelite spies. More than that, she told them she believed that the God of Israel was "the supreme God of the heavens above and the earth below." Wow! She was a friend and a true believer in God.

Sometimes we get caught in the trap of thinking that all people who believe in God will look and act exactly like us. We have to remember that the world is a great big place and that God looks at people differently than we do. God looks at people through eyes of love. God sees their potential. God knows that he built into all people a longing to love God and be loved in return.

Let's each make a "Rahab's Window" craft and see if we can use it to challenge us to look at people differently.

Lead kids to the craft table. Simple instructions for assembly are printed on the handout.

After making the craft, ask:

• **Describe how Rahab helps us see that ★** *anyone can come to God in faith.*

• **How is the way God looks at people different from the way we look at people?**

• **Why do you think there's such a difference?**

COMMITMENT
....

Seeing Through God's Eyes

Ask everyone to look through the window of their completed "Rahab's Window" craft.

Say: **We know that God made each person on earth, loves us, and wants us to love him back. In the same way, he made an emptiness inside us that can only be filled with God's love. In other words, everyone is looking for his love, whether they know it or not!**

Ask:

• **How can looking at people through your Rahab's Window help remind you that everyone is looking for God?**

All Together Now

Rahab's Window

Create a model of Rahab's window to help you look at people in a new way. Follow the directions on the cut-out part of the window to assemble the model. Then look through the window.

How do you see people? Do you see everyone as a person who longs to love God and be loved by him? At first the spies thought Rahab would be their enemy, but then they found out that she loved God, too.

Look through your window and ask God to help you see people in new ways. Love people the way God does this week!

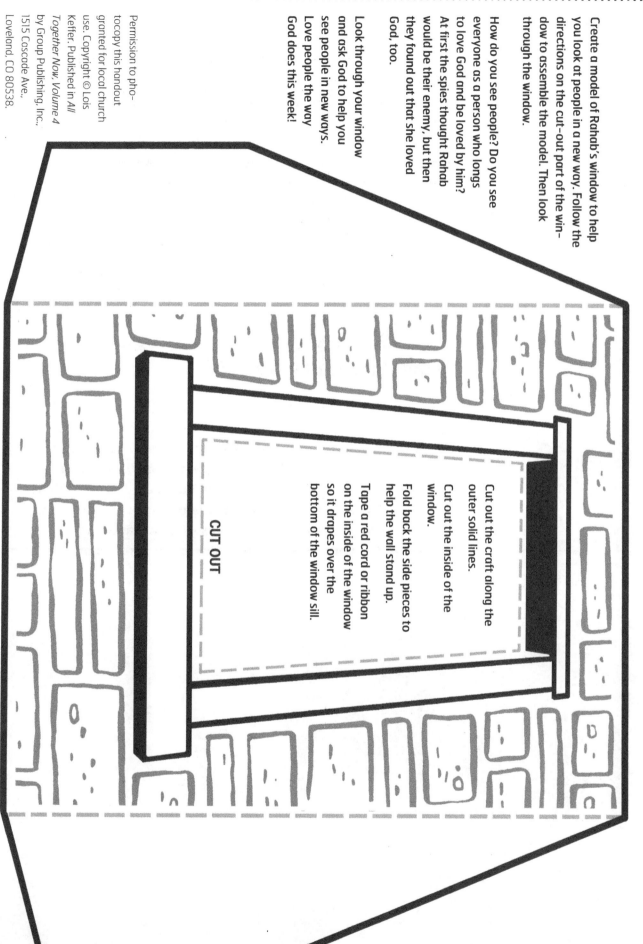

CUT OUT

Cut out the craft along the outer solid lines.

Cut out the inside of the window.

Fold back the side pieces to help the wall stand up.

Tape a red cord or ribbon on the inside of the window so it drapes over the bottom of the window sill.

• How can looking at people through your Rahab's window help you see them differently?

• What's the most important thing you've learned from Rahab's experience?

Say: **The truth is that ★** *anyone can come to God in faith.* **Let's brainstorm some creative ways you can use your Rahab's Windows to remind you of that this week.**

Encourage kids to brainstorm with partners or small groups and then report back to the whole group how they'll use their Rahab's Windows to see others through God's eyes and remember that ★ *anyone can come to God in faith.*

CLOSING
. . . .

Rahab's Window Prayer

Invite kids to form a shoulder-to-shoulder circle and look upward through their Rahab's Windows for the closing prayer.

Pray: **God, we believe that ★** *anyone can come to you in faith.* **Please help us see others the way you do. Help us drop misunderstanding and feelings like jealousy that might keep us from seeing possible Rahabs in our own lives. Give us eyes of love, eyes of mercy, eyes of grace and understanding. Let your love flow through us. In Jesus' name, amen.**

Stones From the River

LESSON AIM

To help kids know that ★ *it's important to remember when God helps us.*

OBJECTIVES

Kids will

✓ go on a treasure hunt for stones,

✓ hear how Joshua had the people make a monument of stones from the Jordan River,

✓ make containers for their own Stones of Remembrance, and

✓ pray about adding to their stone monuments as God works in their lives.

BIBLE BASIS

📖 Joshua 3–4

This passage finds the Israelites about to enter a new era. After 40 years of wandering the desert, conquering the lands of the Transjordan, the Israelites set their faces toward their first hoped-for conquest in the Promised Land itself. Joshua brought them to the edge of the Jordan River to cross it and take their first steps into the Promised Land.

When we look at the Jordan River today, we're tempted to think, so what's the big deal? First, the flow of the Jordan River is far less now than it was even at the beginning of the last century.

You'll need...

☐ 5 river rocks per child (if river rocks aren't available in your area, they're available from craft stores)

☐ snack-size plastic bags for rock gathering

☐ sticky notes

☐ pencils

☐ copy of the Jordan River map (p. 38)

☐ blue crepe paper or holographic streamers

☐ copy of the "Position Flags" handout (p. 39)

☐ scissors

☐ 4 straws

☐ 4 glasses or plastic cups

☐ hole punch

☐ blocks or other small objects to represent the people of Israel

☐ Bible in an easy-to-understand translation

☐ copies of the "Rock Box" handout (p. 43) on heavy paper

☐ permanent markers (use with adult supervision)

☐ glue sticks

☐ raffia

Buy Something (handwritten)

Its tributaries water a dry and thirsty land, and over the years have been dammed to service needy areas, gradually diminishing the amount of water that flows into the Jordan. Second, this Israelite crossing happened during the spring when snowmelt from Mount Hermon had the river at flood stage, swollen far beyond its normal borders, with turbulent currents running swift and deep.

So change your image of the Jordan from the calm, fairly small river you see pictured in the Holy Land to a mighty torrent rushing outside its borders, flooding adjacent areas. The Lord gave Joshua distinct orders for the priests to lead the way carrying the Ark of the Covenant; everyone else was to maintain a distance of approximately one-half mile behind.

The priests' feet touched the edge of the water and the flow stopped. It "[stood] up like a wall" about 17 miles north of their crossing point, and the riverbed stayed dry while the entire nation of Israel crossed. Joshua commanded one man from each of the 12 tribes to heave a stone from the river onto his shoulder and carry it across. Later Joshua created a memorial from these stones so that when children ask, "What do these stones mean?" the answer will be given: " 'They remind us that the Jordan River stopped flowing when the Ark of the Lord's Covenant went across.' These stones will stand as a memorial among the people of Israel forever" (Joshua 4:6-7).

Interestingly, tectonic shifts have caused similar stoppages of the Jordan on other occasions: in 1267, 1906, and 1927, when the river stopped for 21 hours.

When the Israelites arrived at their camping place (called Gilgal), Joshua ordered all the men to be circumcised. After a three-day period of healing, the Israelites celebrated their first Passover in the Promised Land. The next day, manna from heaven ceased to fall. They had entered a new age of living off the land that God had promised to them so long ago.

One of the great themes of the Old Testament is *remembrance.* Remember God's deliverance here. Remember God's provision there. Remember how God struck down enemies. Remember God's mercy and favor.

The practice of remembering included tying Scripture to foreheads or forearms and to the doorposts of houses. It included stacking stones from a miraculously crossed river.

How well it serves us to remember God's faithfulness. We can look to what God has done for us in the past as reassurance that he'll continue to care for us in the future. God's mercies are new every morning.

All Together Now

📖 **2 Thessalonians 2:13-17**

The Israelites arrived in the Promised Land right at harvest time. They were able to harvest the first fruits of the land to present to God for their Passover offerings.

The idea of "first fruits" takes on an interesting new meaning in this passage from 2 Thessalonians. Paul and his companions have planted the seeds of the gospel all over the known world, and in Thessalonica, the Christians represent the first fruits of their labor for God.

No longer are memorials made of standing stones, but of people built into the living church—people whose faithfulness brought the gospel forward more than 2,000 years so that we might share in its glorious knowledge today.

UNDERSTANDING YOUR KIDS

Your first fruits are in the young lives you touch each week. I know there are weeks you go home tearing your hair, wondering if one word you said got through. It does. Believe me, it does.

It's fascinating to sit down with a group of adults and ask them about the first encounter with Jesus they can remember. Time after time I'll hear, "There was this one Sunday school teacher..."

Though physical disability has kept me from teaching in person for the last few years, I love encountering one of my former kids in a church hallway. There'll be a quick intake of breath, a big smile, and the welcome exclamation, "Mrs. Lois!"

Or sometimes it'll just be a knee hug from a former student's younger sibling. These are precious monuments, first fruits, if you will. I know that teaching can be very frustrating for many reasons. But those first fruits *are* coming. Your calm and grace-filled presence makes a huge difference in kids. You're building a living memorial to God's faithfulness in young lives. And some of them will in turn do the same.

There's absolutely no greater calling!

THE LESSON »

ATTENTION GRABBER

Treasure Hunt!

As kids arrive, greet them warmly and give them snack-size plastic bags for the treasure hunt to come.

Say: **We're going on a treasure hunt! Before we can begin, let's see if you can guess what we're hunting for.**

To help kids come up with *rocks,* give clues such as they're usually on the ground, they're hard, they can be black or white or lots of colors in between, they can be sharp or smooth, or sometimes bugs hide underneath them.

Say: **We're not looking for any old rocks, mind you. We need rocks that are big enough to write something on them.**

Show kids one or two rocks of appropriate size.

Say: **Please remember the size of these rocks—too large or too small won't work. Gather three to five treasure rocks, but no more than five.** Tell kids if they find more than five of the right size, they can share with others.

Ask one of the kids to repeat the instructions back to you, and then lead your young treasure hunters to their hunting site.

As kids search, let them know if the rocks they find will work. Encourage those who have found all their rocks to help others. Gather everyone to make sure their treasure bags have three to five rocks before you return to the room together.

In your meeting area, have kids set their rocks along a wall where they'll be out of the way. Have them label their rocks with their names jotted on sticky notes.

Say: **You're probably wondering about how we'll use our treasure rocks. I can tell you this much: We'll use them for a very important purpose. But I can't tell you exactly what until after our Bible passage. Or perhaps you'll get some clues about their purpose during the Bible passage.**

I will tell you that today we're going to learn that ★ *it's important to remember when God helps us.* **The Israelites are about to experience one of those moments. And let me tell you, it's a** *great moment!* **Come on, let's find out what happens!**

Prep Box

The opening rock treasure hunt can be done inside or outside. If there are rocks in the landscaping around your building, let kids hunt for them outside. If not, purchase river rocks and hide them in as large an area of the church as is available to you.

Teacher Tip

If you're taking kids outside for their treasure hunt, give instructions to keep them in one area so you'll have eyes on all of them at one time. If you're going to move to another side of the church to hunt, do so as a group. You may want to recruit a couple extra adult volunteers for the hunt. Keep an eye on your time so your hunt doesn't exceed 10 minutes.

All Together Now

BIBLE EXPLORATION

Stones From the River (Joshua 3–4)

Say: **God's people, the Israelites, were ready to turn a new page in their history. More than 40 years ago, Moses had led them out of slavery in Egypt. They crossed a great desert and came to the land God had promised them. At that time, Moses sent 12 spies into the Promised Land to check it out. Two of the spies came back saying, "Let's go in and take the land right now!" But the other 10 warned, "The people are like giants—we could never conquer them." God was so disappointed with the people's lack of faith that he turned them right back toward the desert and told them they would have to wander in the desert for 40 years. By that time, the unfaithful people would have died.**

Forty years passed. The 10 unfaithful spies had died. Moses and the two faithful spies, Joshua and Caleb, were still alive. Let's set up the room so we can see what happened next.

Display the Jordan River map. Have kids run a length of blue crepe paper across the middle of your room and stack chairs at the "north" end to represent Mount Hermon. Have them use crepe paper to outline the Sea of Galilee and the Dead Sea as shown on the map and then fill in the seas with torn crepe paper.

While kids are filling the seas, ask for two kids to prepare the position flags. Give them a copy of the "Position Flags" handout, scissors, pencils, four straws, and four glasses or plastic cups. Have them each cut out two position flags, punch holes in the circles on the flags, and then weave straws through the holes. Have kids stand the flags in glasses or stand them by poking holes in the bottoms of plastic cups and pushing the flag straws through the holes.

Help your flag creators place their flags in approximately the correct positions along the crepe paper Jordan River.

Say: **This long blue line you've created stands for the Jordan River. These position flags mark important places in today's Scripture. But first let me fill you in on what's already happened.**

Explain to kids that Moses brought the Israelites all the way up the far side of the Jordan River (indicate the "east" side), and conquered all the nations along the way. Then he brought everyone back to the middle, and they camped at Acacia Grove. That's where Moses died and Joshua took over.

ACACIA GROVE

Teacher Tip

If you've gathered rocks outside, return via a church kitchen or restroom where kids can quickly rinse their rocks clean.

Jordan River Map

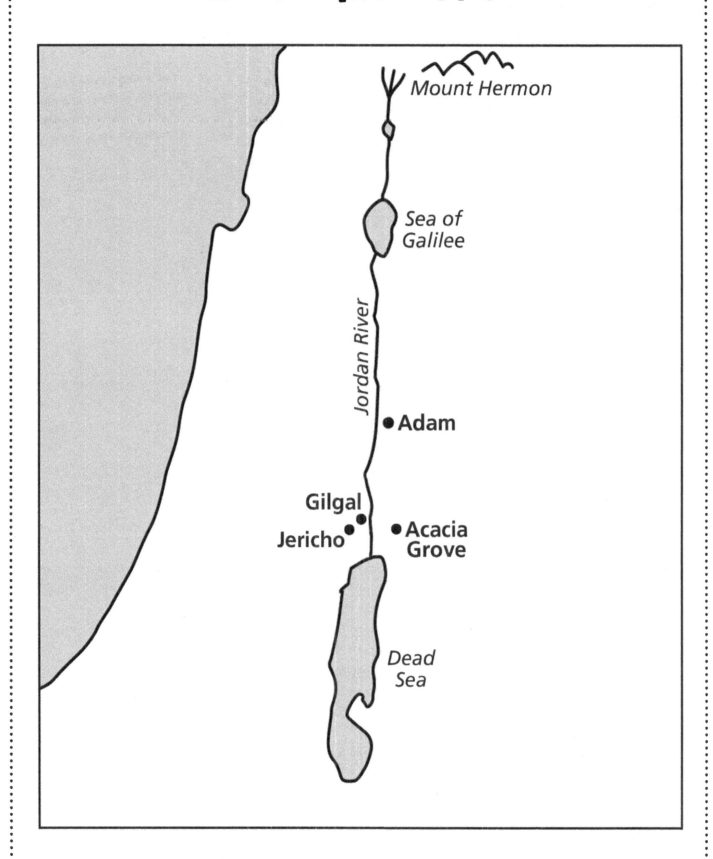

Mount Hermon

Sea of Galilee

Jordan River

● Adam

Gilgal

Jericho ● Acacia Grove

Dead Sea

Position Flags

Cut out the four position flags. Punch a hole in each of the [...]
Weave a pencil or straw through the circles. Your flags are re[...]

ACACIA GROVE

GILGAL

JERICHO

ADAM

Put on cards

Published in *All Together Now, Volume 4* by Group Publishing, Inc., 1515 Cascade Ave., Loveland, CO 80538.

39

Ask volunteers to place blocks or other small objects at Acacia Grove to represent the Israelite people.

Say: **The Promised Land the Israelites really wanted was on the other side of the Jordan River. That's where Joshua planned his first attack. He sent his spies into Jericho where Rahab helped them. Finally, it was time to get everyone ready to take the big step of crossing the Jordan River and stepping into the Promised Land for the very first time.**

***But* it was early spring. What happens to rivers in the spring?**

Snow from way up there on Mount Hermon (point to the pile of chairs at the "north" end of the river) **melted and filled the Jordan until it flooded. Between the melting snow and the winter rains, the Jordan River went from a medium-sized river to a wide, flooding torrent with dangerous currents flowing far outside its usual banks.**

Have a few kids use more crepe paper to make the Jordan much wider.

Say: **It certainly doesn't look like a river that could be crossed! But God gave Joshua special instructions. God said to have the priests go first, carrying the Ark of the Covenant. The Ark of the Covenant was the special box that held the stone tablets of the Ten Commandments.**

God promised that as soon as the priests' feet touched the water, the river would dry up and everyone would be able to cross on dry ground. So Joshua gave God's instructions and the priests marched ahead.

Assign two kids to arrange four blocks with another block on top of them to represent the priests carrying the Ark of the Covenant. Have them move the blocks right to the edge of the crepe paper river.

Ask:

• **What do you think happened when the priests' feet touched the water?**

Say: **God kept his word. The river backed up as far as Adam and piled up there in a great wall of water.**

Assign two volunteers to pull the crepe paper river as far back as the position flag at Adam.

Say: **The priests with the Ark of the Covenant stepped forward on dry ground to the middle of the riverbed and stood there while all the Israelites passed over.**

Assign other kids to move the blocks accordingly.

Say: **Joshua told one man from each of the 12 tribes to**

All Together Now

pick up a large rock from the middle of the river bed and carry it on his shoulder to the other side. Finally, the priests carrying the Ark of the Covenant crossed the river.

Assign kids to move the blocks representing the priests and the Ark of the Covenant.

Say: **As soon as the priests stepped out of the river bed, the water came rushing back down.**

Have kids put the crepe paper river back into place.

Say: **Joshua led all the Israelites to their new camping place at Gilgal.**

Have kids move all the blocks near the position flag at Gilgal.

Say: **That night Joshua took the 12 stones from the middle of the river and set them up as a memorial in the camp. Here's what he said to the people.**

Ask a willing child to read Joshua 4:21-24.

Say: **So with the help of a great miracle from God, the Israelites crossed the Jordan and spent their first night in the Promised Land!**

Thank you all for helping tell the story with all these props!

Ask:

• What do you think it would be like to cross a flooding river on dry ground?

• What do the stones that came from the river represent to you?

Say: **Here and in many other places, the Bible teaches us that ★** *it's important to remember when God helps us.* **These stones from the river reminded the Israelites of God's great miracle in helping them cross the flooded Jordan River on dry ground.**

Now it's your turn to remember moments when God has helped you.

LIFE APPLICATION
. . . .
Stones of Remembrance

Explain to kids that they're going to write reminders of times God did great things for them on the stones they collected.

Ask:

• What are some things God has done for you in your life—something you want to remember?

If kids have trouble coming up with ideas, mention things such as keeping them safe in a big storm, helping a sick family member get better, helping them make friends after a move, answering a prayer they'd been praying for a long time. Once you've primed the discussion, encourage kids to come up with even more ideas.

Ask:

• **How does remembering these times encourage you?**

Challenge kids to think of two or three times God helped them that they want to remember. Then help them reduce their thoughts to just a couple of words. Have them use permanent markers to write those words on their rocks. Be on hand to do the writing for kids who would like your assistance.

Say: **Most of you have extra rocks. That's good! You can use them for future times God helps you. These stones are just the beginning of your Stones of Remembrance collection. If you want to, you can keep adding to the collection your whole life, because ★ it's important to remember when God helps us.**

COMMITMENT

. . . .

Rock Box

Say: **Now all you need is a holder for your special Stones of Remembrance!**

Lead kids to your craft area. You'll find simple instructions for completing the Rock Box printed on the handout. As kids finish, have them clean up their paper clippings and then offer to help other kids who may need a hand with weaving and tying the raffia knot.

Have kids place their Stones of Remembrance in their Rock Boxes and join you in a discussion circle.

Ask:

• **How's your making this collection of stones like Joshua bringing stones out of the Jordan River?**

• **Why is it ★ important to remember when God helps us?**

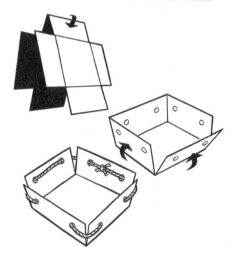

Prep Box

Make a sample Rock Box to show the kids. Set out copies of the "Rock Box" handout (p. 43) printed on heavy paper, scissors, glue sticks, a hole punch, and raffia.

All Together Now

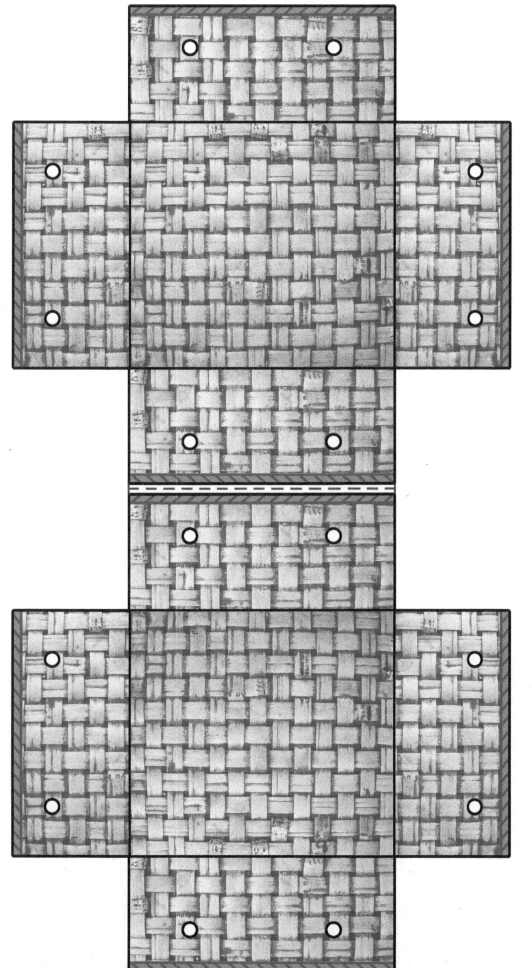

Rock Box

Fold the pattern on the dotted line. Line up the edges carefully, and then cut them out together. Use a glue stick to firmly seal the layers together. Then fold up the sides, and use a hole punch to punch holes where the circles are. Fold a long strand of raffia in half, and weave the double strand through the holes to hold the box together. Knot the ends together on the inside. Voilà! You have a box for your Stones of Remembrance.

Prayer of Remembrance

Say: **Let's give thanks to God for all he's done for us. I'll pause in my prayer. All at the same time, you can say out loud one thing you wrote on your Stones of Remembrance. Then I'll finish the prayer.**

Pray: **Dear Lord, we know that ★** *it's important to remember when you help us.* **Today we've written on our Stones of Remembrance these ways you've helped us in the past.** Pause as children insert their ideas. **Our faith is in you, Lord. We trust our lives to you and believe we'll be writing on many more Stones of Remembrance in the future. In Jesus' name, amen.**

The Walls Go Tumblin' Down

LESSON AIM

To help kids know that ★ *we can always trust God's instructions.*

OBJECTIVES

Kids will

✓ follow strange instructions to earn a treat,

✓ recreate the collapse of Jericho's walls in three acts,

✓ make a pop-up of Jericho's walls, and

✓ commit to following God's instructions.

BIBLE BASIS

 Joshua 5:13–6:27

The book of Joshua is full of Joshua's amazing feats as the leader of the Israelite army. The battle of Jericho stands out as most people's favorite Bible passage regarding Joshua. Perhaps it has something to do with the terrific song written about it. Perhaps it's because the conquest of Jericho was the first in the Promised Land. Perhaps it's because God's instructions for the conquest were so strange—they were given to highlight the fact that God alone was truly the conqueror. Or perhaps it's some combination of the three that makes the conquest of Jericho the stuff of which irresistible tales are made.

Jericho was already an ancient city when Joshua arrived. Situated at 800 feet below sea level, this "City of Palms" was a haven

You'll need...

☐ simple snack, such as fresh strawberries or doughnut holes*

☐ cardboard, hardboard, or taped newspaper base for building Jericho

☐ markers

☐ whiteboard or newsprint

☐ several dozen foam or plastic cups

☐ copies of "And the Walls Go Down!" handout (p. 53)

☐ scissors

☐ glue sticks

* Always check for allergies before serving snacks.

from the wintry winds of Jerusalem, though Jerusalem sat just 17 miles to the southwest. Various excavations of the site of ancient Jericho beginning in 1867 have allowed the original ruins to be damaged by erosion, but a quick search online for significant digs around the area will reveal a forbidding round tower that formed part of the city's ruined walls. Though we don't know the exact configuration of Jericho's defenses, rows of collapsed and crushed stone and earthen embankments suggest they were formidable.

The exact site of the Israelite encampment of Gilgal is unknown, but some conjecture is that it must have been about two miles northeast of Jericho. Since Jericho wasn't far from the Jordan River, the large Israelite encampment would surely have been close enough to inspire even greater fear in the hearts of the already frightened people of Jericho. The population at Gilgal contained most of the Israelite nation—probably at least 1,000,000 people. Jericho was but one city of unknown population. Its people had every reason to be quaking in fear—not simply from the uneven numbers, but from the fact that the Israelites served the living God.

God's instructions for marching around the wall for six days also called for human silence except the sounding of the shofar, or ram's horn trumpet. I never realized what a stirring instrument this was until I sat in a day-long seminar with a Hebrew teacher and he sounded the shofar as part of a call to prayer. Enrich your understanding of this Bible passage by looking up *shofar* on YouTube and listening to it being sounded by a skilled player. As the soldiers marched in silence around the Ark of the Covenant, seven priests continually sounded their shofars. On the seventh day, the shofars sounded during each of seven circuits around the city. The Israelite army followed God's strange instructions exactly, and on the seventh day when Joshua finally gave the command to shout, the collapse of the wall was entirely God's work.

📖 Hebrews 11:30

Perhaps those soldiers silently marching were not merely marching, but praying as well! For because of this, they find themselves enshrined in the Bible's famous hall of fame, Hebrews 11. "It was by faith that the people of Israel marched around Jericho for seven days, and the walls came crashing down" (Hebrews 11:30).

After all, the people of Israel had just seen God stop the waters of Jordan at flood stage so they could cross into the Promised Land on dry ground. This event caused them to revere Joshua as they had Moses. It reminded them that theirs was a living God who was operating on their behalf.

Marching and praying can work for you, too. By faith you can pray for God to guide your driving. By faith you pray all through the week for an effective Sunday school class. Join the heroes and heroines of Hebrews 11. Whatever you do, do it by faith and watch God work!

UNDERSTANDING YOUR KIDS

Following instructions isn't always number one on kids' happy list. Try getting them to stop playing a favorite game, and you're likely to hear a concert of grumbles and groans. Or if you call time on an activity when they feel they need just a few more minutes to complete it, you may hear some cranky voices as well. Waiting three minutes to get a drink or take a bathroom break—are you kidding?

Even more than adults, kids love it when instructions coincide with the way they're feeling at that moment. That's why one of your jobs as a teacher is to make each lesson activity sound as exciting as ice cream bars on a hot summer day. Set the stage with a teaser that heightens kids' curiosity. Weave each new activity into the previous one and the one that follows. Make sure that kids see how the Bible point applies to their lives and that they have a good plan for carrying it out as they head into the week.

Keep your own face bright and shiny no matter how you're feeling, enter each lesson with enthusiasm and a twinkle in your eye, use humor as your faithful sidekick, and suddenly you'll find kids falling all over themselves to follow your instructions.

THE LESSON »

Say What?

Greet kids warmly and warn them that there may be strange goings-on today. When everyone has arrived, form two groups, making sure that you have an equal number of younger and older kids in each group.

Say: **It's such a lovely day, I think we ought to have a snowman-building contest. Who says we can't build snowmen in the summer?**

Lead kids to an outdoor spot. If it happens to be raining, lead them to a covered porch.

Say: **The rules of this contest are quite simple. You'll have two minutes to build your snowmen. They must be made of a large snowball on the bottom, a middle-sized snowball in the middle, and a smaller one for the head. Don't forget to add features on the face. At the end of two minutes, I'll call time and the group that built the best snowman will get a yummy treat. There will be no questions today. Simply start building your snowmen when I say "go." Go!**

No matter how much the kids object or how strangely they look at you, steadfastly look at your watch or cell phone. Keep an eye out for kids who actually pretend to build snowmen. Let kids discuss your strange instructions amongst themselves.

Call time after two minutes, and give what sounds like legitimate critiques of the snowmen. For instance, you might say you admire the symmetry of the large building balls on one and the facial details on the other. Or you might like one's hat and scarf and another's carrot nose and button eyes. If kids catch on to your imaginary critiques, let them make their own comments as well.

Finally, say: **Well, I hate to mention this, but our lovely snowmen are starting to melt. I hate to leave them here like this because you put such good work into them, but here's my final judgment: The contest is a tie. Everyone wins a treat!**

Lead kids quietly back to your meeting room and serve the treat you've prepared.

Ask:

• **Describe what it was like to follow my instructions for snowman building.**

• **Why did you or why didn't you play along with my little game?**

Prep Box

Hide a small snack, such as fresh strawberries or doughnut holes, in your room.

All Together Now

Say: **It was pretty funny to watch your faces as I gave you crazy instructions! I'm glad you trusted me enough to play along—or at least that you were hungry enough to play along! I may have given you silly instructions, but today we're going to learn that ★** *we can always trust God's instructions.*

God's instructions don't always make a lot of sense to us—at least in the middle of a situation. Later we can look back and see that God told us just the right thing to do.

That's exactly what happened to the Israelites when they were ready to attack Jericho. God gave Joshua a battle plan, and then Joshua passed on the plan to his army. It might be just about the strangest battle plan you've ever heard, but the Israelites knew it was God's plan, so they followed it.

Let's discover a little more about this plan.

BIBLE EXPLORATION

Taking Jericho: The Battle in Three Acts

(Joshua 5:13–6:27)

Say: **We'll find that the Bible tells about this event in three parts. In the first part, Joshua encounters a strange man. In the second part, Joshua gets instructions from God.**

Let's stay in our snowman-building groups. Indicate one of the groups as Group 1. **Group 1, please read Joshua 5:13-15 and prepare a skit to show what happened.**

Group 2, please read Joshua 6:1-5. Prepare a step-by-step illustration to explain God's strange instructions. You'll have about five minutes to prepare. Go for it!

Give Group 2 markers and a whiteboard or large sheets of newsprint.

After five minutes call time and have both groups give their presentations. After both groups have presented, allow kids to ask questions of those in the other group.

Ask:

• **What do you think it would be like to meet the commander of God's army standing in front of you with his sword drawn?**

• **Describe what you think of Joshua's reaction to this mighty warrior.**

Review River + Stones + crossing the Jordan. p. 40 (handwritten)

Prep Box

Prepare a base for the Jericho the kids are going to build from cups. Use a large sheet of cardboard or hardboard, or tape several sheets of newspaper together to form a large working surface.

I read students act it out. Then watch video. (handwritten)

Say: **When Joshua became the leader of the Israelites, God told him to be strong and courageous—God promised to always be with him if Joshua followed God's ways. And so far Joshua had done that. But now Joshua was going into battle and he was about to hear some very strange instructions.**

Ask:

• **What do you think about the military instructions Joshua got from God?**

• **How would you decide whether to obey the strange instructions?**

Say: **You've done a great job telling the first two parts of this event! Now let's all get together to tell the third part.**

Gather the kids around the cardboard, hardboard, or newspaper base you've prepared for the building of Jericho. Set out foam or plastic cups.

Explain to kids that archaeological digs at the site of Jericho tell us that it was already an ancient city when Joshua and the Israelites arrived there. It had massively thick and high walls that no one could hope to climb or tear down.

Say: **As you see, I've provided a base for you to build a model of the city with these cups. Turn the cups upside down for building. Form your city wall into an oval shape, and then build it about four cups high. You'll need to work together.**

Have kids choose a Building Captain to direct the building process, a Row Checker to make sure each row of the wall is sturdy, and a Crew Organizer to see that everyone gets an equal chance to participate in the building of the city wall. Once these positions are filled, let kids enjoy the process of planning and building their very own model of Jericho's city walls.

When kids have used most of the cups, invite them to use a few extra to make slightly taller watchtowers at four places around the wall. Ask the Crew Organizer to do a final inspection, and then give your approval.

Say: **OK, we need a little guidance from Group 2. What are our instructions for taking this city?**

Let members of Group 2 remind you that everyone needs to march around the city once a day for six days with the priests carrying the Ark of the Covenant and the trumpets blowing. Ask for four volunteers to carry a pretend Ark of the Covenant. Let the rest of the kids be trumpet blowers.

Set up your marchers in a circle well beyond the borders of your

All Together Now

model city. Have them march around the city once and then sit down while you turn off the lights. After a moment, turn the lights back on. Repeat until you've done this six times.

Then say: **OK, this is the big day! We've followed God's strange instructions and marched in faith. Forward one more time! On the seventh time around, when I say "Shout!" you will shout, "For the Lord!" and raise your sword arms. Let's march!**

When you cry "Shout!" bump the base of the model city wall with your foot. Motion for kids to do the same. Immediately your wall will come down. Give a mighty round of applause when it does. Then invite kids to join you sitting around the ruins of your city.

Say: **When the horns blew and the people shouted, the great walls of Jericho fell straight down. They just collapsed—poof! So the Israelite soldiers marched straight in and conquered the city.**

But one part of the city wall stood firm. Ask if kids can figure out what part of the wall that was. It's OK if kids are stumped by this question.

Say: **From one window in the city wall there hung a scarlet cord. Joshua told his soldiers to go in and rescue everyone in that house. It was the house of Rahab, who'd helped the Israelites.**

Say: **That very night Rahab and her family made their own campsite outside the large Israelite camp. Every member of Rahab's family was saved.**

Ask:

• **Now that all of this has happened, what do you think of God's strange battle plan?**

Say: **Of course we can never know exactly what is in God's mind unless he tells us. But we know that ★** *we can always trust God's instructions.* **Maybe God gives us instructions that seem a little strange just to show us his power, so that we'll learn to trust him in the future.**

Teacher Tip

Consider enhancing the experience by playing the sound of a shofar from a laptop computer or MP3 device.

LIFE APPLICATION
. . . .

Who You Gonna Trust?

Ask:

• **Describe some instructions we have from God.**

Say: **One instruction we sometimes struggle with is loving our enemies. That's an instruction from God that seems kind of strange. Jesus told us to love our enemies and do good to people who want to harm us.**

Ask:

• **Explain whether that seems strange to you.**

• **How about Jesus' instruction to turn the other cheek when someone slaps us rather than getting back at that person?**

• **What do you think about Jesus' instruction to take the least important place at the table or in the room, allowing others to take the more important seats?**

Encourage kids to discuss their feelings about following each of these challenging instructions from Jesus.

Say: **Even though these aren't things we'd naturally do and they might seem kind of strange to us, they're still God's instructions.**

Ask:

• **How could us following these instructions accomplish good things for God's kingdom?**

Say: **No one ever said following God's instructions would be easy, but as we see from what happened at Jericho, ★ *we can always trust God's instructions*. And when we obey God with faith in our hearts, we can count on God to do great things.**

COMMITMENT
. . . .

And the Walls Go Down!

Lead kids to your craft area.

Ask:

• **So, how did the walls of Jericho fall down?**

• **Describe whether you believe this story—and why.**

Say: **What happened at Jericho is true—because it's in the Bible. I believe what's in the Bible. And I believe that ★ *we can always trust God's instructions*. Now, how about if you follow my instructions to make this cool Jericho pop-up? When you have it made, you can make the walls of Jericho fall down any time you want to!**

The directions for making the pop-up are printed on the handout. Kids will be cutting the handout and the directions apart, so they're reprinted on page 54 for your convenience.

Prep Box

Make a sample "And the Walls Go Down!" pop-up for kids to see. Set out copies of the "And the Walls Go Down!" hand-out (p. 53), scissors, and glue sticks.

And the Walls Go Down!

With your own pop-up model of Jericho, you can make the walls go down on command!

1. Cut out the two large pieces on the heavy outer lines.
2. The bottom piece is the background. Fold it in half to close it; then open it again.
3. Fold back on all the dotted lines on the city wall piece.
4. Glue the top and bottom tabs of the city wall to the rectangles on the background.

5. Curve the side pieces to form towers that bump out. Glue the last sections to the backs of the first sections of the towers.
6. When you flatten the background, the walls fall down!

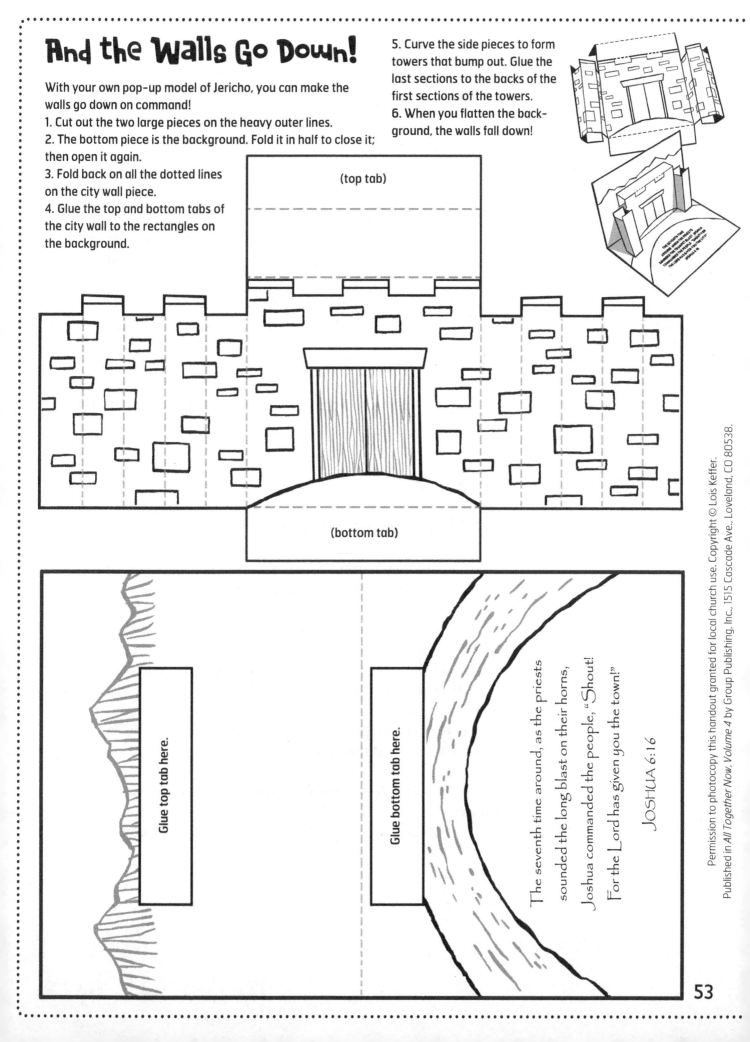

(top tab)

(bottom tab)

Glue top tab here.

Glue bottom tab here.

The seventh time around, as the priests sounded the long blast on their horns, Joshua commanded the people, "*Shout!* For the Lord has given you the town!"

JOSHUA 6:16

Published in *All Together Now, Volume 4* by Group Publishing, Inc., 1515 Cascade Ave., Loveland, CO 80538.

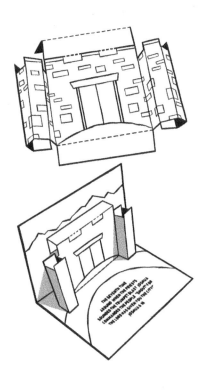

✓ Cut out the two large pieces on the heavy lines.

✓ The bottom piece is the background. Fold it in half to close it; then open it again.

✓ Fold back on all the dotted lines on the city wall piece.

✓ Glue the top and bottom tabs of the city wall to the rectangles on the background.

✓ Curve the side pieces to form towers that bump out. Glue the last sections to the backs of the first sections of the towers.

✓ When you flatten the background, the walls fall down!

Have kids clean up the craft area as they finish, and offer to help kids who could use another pair of hands to complete their projects.

Then gather kids in a circle with their pop-ups and ask:

• **How can these pop-ups help us remember to follow God's instructions?**

• **Who's one person you can share today's Bible passage with this week?**

CLOSING

Wall-Crushing Power

Say: **God isn't someone we see with our eyes, so it's easy to forget that he has wall-crushing power. God's instructions are written in the Bible for us not only to see, but also to know and understand. We can open our Bibles every day and read what God wants for us. In fact, reading the Word every day was one of God's original instructions to Joshua.**

Hold out your Bible.

Say: **If you would like to know more about God's instructions for your life, read a little bit of this book every day. It's packed full of all the good stuff God wants you to know.**

Ask:

• **Do you believe that ★ *we can always trust God's instructions*?**

Say: **Then go out into your world and have a good week!**

All Together Now

Deborah-Barak-Jael—Oh, My!

You'll need...

- ☐ slips of paper
- ☐ pen
- ☐ a copy of "Names" (p. 59)
- ☐ scissors
- ☐ hole punch
- ☐ yarn
- ☐ copies of "Deborah's Script" (p. 61), "Barak's Script (p. 62), and "Jael's Script" (p. 63)
- ☐ copies of the "All Kinds of People" handout (p. 65) on heavy paper
- ☐ curling ribbon
- ☐ gummy bears*

* Always check for allergies before serving snacks.

LESSON AIM

To help kids see that ★ *God invites all kinds of people into his kingdom.*

OBJECTIVES

Kids will

- ✓ pantomime the occupation of the Bible passage's three main people,
- ✓ participate in a trio reading of the Bible passage,
- ✓ create an All Kinds of People box with a challenge to be a kingdom changer, and
- ✓ plan ways to be ready to be kingdom changers for God.

BIBLE BASIS

 Judges 4:1–5:31

Meet Deborah, perhaps the greatest prophetess in Israel's history. Deborah is unique in that she's the only prophetess who is not attached to a great man. Given the patriarchal nature of Israelite society, this passage comes as something of a surprise. Or does it? The Old Testament is sprinkled with stories of outstanding women who made a difference in God's kingdom: Sarah, Miriam, Rahab, Ruth, Huldah, and Esther to name just a few. And before this passage is over we'll meet another: Jael.

During Joshua's conquest of Canaan, he conquered cities, but did not stay long enough to drive out the rural population. That duty fell to the tribes who were assigned to each territory. Most of the tribes failed to comply with God's plan. Instead, they intermarried with the Canaanite people, resulting in widespread worship of Baal and Ashtoreth.

Because worship of these pagan gods involved fertility rites and ritual prostitution, these evolved into common practices among those who were supposed to be the people of the Living God. These behaviors not only broke God's heart, but incurred his wrath. During periods of disobedience and consorting with pagan gods, God allowed other countries to overrun Israel and bring great hardship upon its people. And so it went during the roughly 400-year period of the judges.

Judges 4 tells us that Deborah sat as a judge under a great palm tree and settled people's arguments. Hers was not a litigious court as today's are. She would have been more of a wise adviser. In chapter 5 she calls herself "a mother for Israel."

During this time, the Israelites were constantly harassed by peoples of the plains who were skilled at working with iron. The plains people had iron chariots and weapons, far superior to the weaponry of the Israelites, who were forced to live in the hill country.

When God told Deborah to send Barak (BAY-rak), the mightiest military man of the time, against Sisera's chariots, it must have seemed to Barak like a suicide mission. But he should have known God would be with them. Judges 5:21 tells us that Sisera's people were swept away by a torrent. The ancient historian Josephus wrote of such heavy rain, hail, and flooding that the Canaanites were unable to use their superior weaponry. Confronted by the ferocity of the Israelites who had faith that God was behind the weather, Sisera's army fell into terrified confusion and ended up trampling and running over many of their own.

Barak sought Deborah's presence at the battle—not necessarily because he was cowardly, but likely because he wanted her insight. It was common for prophets to be present at battles to assure God's presence and to advise. It was in these roles that Deborah served, not as a warrior. On Mount Tabor, prior to the battle, Deborah announced the victory (Judges 4:14), giving Barak confidence to take on Sisera's superior forces.

Those who spend years studying Hebrew tell us how much we miss in not understanding the significance of Hebrew names. This passage is a great example. *Deborah* means "bee." In this case she was the queen bee who rallied the swarm for battle and stung the enemy. Her second name, *Lappidoth*, means "torches." *Barak* means "lightning." Deborah is the *torch* to Barak's *lightning*. Nice!

But the real heroine is Jael (JAY-el), whose name means

All Together Now

mountain goat. When Sisera saw that defeat was imminent, he ran to the tent of Jael, wife of Heber the Kenite. The Kenites were distant relatives of the Israelites through Moses' father-in-law Jethro. So though there were trade relations with Sisera's people, the Kenites' main loyalty was clearly with the Israelites. There are many interpretations of what happened when Sisera entered Jael's tent. At first blush, it looks like premeditated murder on Jael's part. But Deborah's poem seems to indicate a struggle.

It is hard to judge what happened in an ancient culture, especially when it's recorded in an equally ancient and sometimes hard-to-decipher language. The Jews consider Jael to be a savior of their nation, reasoning that she could not have defended herself against a heavily armed, trained warrior when she was alone and defenseless in her tent. Her killing of Sisera gave the Israelite culture a chance to recover and flourish once again, under Deborah's wise guidance.

 **Galatians 3:27-29**

This famous passage in Galatians was a game-changer for the early church, and has ongoing implications for God's people today—even for God's kids! It breaks down barriers between all kinds of people: Jew and Gentile, slaves and free, male and female. How about adults and kids? Kids can be great "operatives" in God's kingdom, especially when they're trained from an early age to believe that they're precious in God's sight and that God's hand is continually upon them.

God bless the churches that take their kids seriously, for they are today's *and* tomorrow's kingdom changers.

UNDERSTANDING YOUR KIDS

The messages kids hear about themselves during their formative years have tremendous, life-long impact. Teaching kids that they can play an important role in God's kingdom *right now* is no small message. Nor is it a made-up esteem builder. Scripture is full of situations where God takes the unlikeliest people and helps them do great things.

You may have kids in your ministry who hear negative messages about themselves all week. Others may hear encouraging words at home, but their tender young selves are looking for affirmation in God's truth. And that truth is, they're not *just* kids, they're God's unique creation, specially designed for service in his kingdom.

Use this lesson to teach kids that God uses all kinds of people in his kingdom—including kids.

THE LESSON »

ATTENTION GRABBER

Who Am I?

As kids arrive, greet each one warmly and by name. Have them form three groups. (A group may be as small as one person.)

Say: **Today we're going to learn that ★ *God invites all kinds of people into his kingdom*. And I mean *all* kinds of people. The three main people in today's Bible passage are just about the unlikeliest group of people you could put together. Let's have each group act out the occupation of one of the three people from today's Bible passage.**

Give a slip of paper with an occupation to each group. Allow a minute for groups to brainstorm how they'll act out their person's occupation for the other groups to guess. Drop by the groups and offer ideas as needed. Then let the pantomimes begin.

Congratulate the groups on their pantomimes, and then say: **Wow! What would a judge, a soldier, and a housewife have to do with each other in a Bible passage? Pretty strange combination, isn't it? I guess we're just going to have to get right into the Bible passage to find out how God used these three people to help his kingdom here on earth.**

BIBLE EXPLORATION

Judge, Soldier, Housewife (Judges 4:1–5:31)

Say: **We're about to jump through a time warp to a different part of Israel's history. Our hero Joshua lived a good long life. As long as he led the army of God, Israel's borders expanded, the people obeyed God, and God blessed them. When Joshua was an old man, he gathered people from all the tribes of Israel and reminded them of all God had done for them. He told them that if they served God, they would live in peace, but if they served fake gods, the living God of Israel would no longer take care of them. Then he made this really famous statement that you may have heard before: "Choose today whom you will serve...But as for me and my family, we will serve the Lord"** (Joshua 24:15). **All the people proclaimed, "We will serve the Lord!"**

Let's all shout that together: We will serve the Lord!

All Together Now

Names

DEBORAH

BARAK

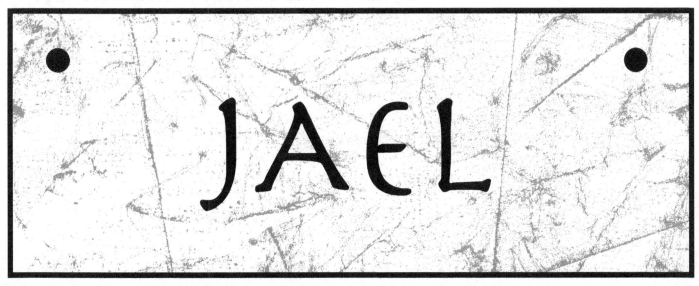

JAEL

Published in *All Together Now, Volume 4* by Group Publishing, Inc., 1515 Cascade Ave., Loveland, CO 80538.

Prep Box

Choose three fluent readers. Give them the Deborah (girl), Barak (boy), and Jael (girl) scripts to become familiar with. You may want to call your readers the night before and ask them to arrive a bit early.

Cut the name tags apart from the copy of the "Names" handout (p. 59), punch holes on the black circles, and tie a length of yarn through the circles so the signs hang comfortably around kids' necks.

After Joshua died, the people had no great leader. Before you knew it, they began to worship fake gods.

Ask:

• **What do you think happens when people worship fake gods?**

Say: **When the people Joshua led stopped following God, God stopped blessing them. Other powerful nations grew up around them and made all kinds of trouble for them. Other nations stole their land and their crops and even made it hard for them to travel from town to town without being robbed.**

Each time this happened, God called a special person, a judge, to guide the people back to God and help get them out of trouble. The judges watched over Israel for about 400 years. That's a lot of years and a lot of judges. Today we're going to hear about just one judge. Her name is Deborah. I've asked [name] **to be our Deborah today.**

Hang the Deborah name tag on the person.

Say: **Our soldier will be** [name] **and our housewife** [name].

Hang the appropriate name tags on Barak and Jael.

Say: **Now, Deborah, Barak, and Jael will tell you what happened. Listen carefully, because it's exciting, and you won't want to miss a word!** Have your child volunteers read their scripts in the following order: Deborah, Barak, Jael.

When Jael has finished reading her script, lead your kids in a great round of applause for all your readers. Then gather everyone in a circle for discussion.

Ask:

• **Why did Barak want Deborah, the woman of God, to go with the soldiers on the day of battle?**

• **How did God show that he was fighting for the Israelites?**

• **How did today's passage demonstrate that ★** *God invites all kinds of people into his kingdom?*

LIFE APPLICATION
....

All Kinds of People Box

Lead kids to your craft area and show kids your completed "All Kinds of People" pyramid box.

Prep Box

Prepare an "All Kinds of People" pyramid box for kids to see. Set out copies of the "All Kinds of People" handout (p. 65), scissors, a hole punch, and a roll of curling ribbon.

All Together Now

Deborah's Script

I'm Deborah, the only woman judge in Israel's history. When I say "judge," you might think of someone who sits in a courtroom with a gavel and says "guilty" or "not guilty." That's not what I was like at all.

I would sit under a great palm tree and listen to people's problems. God would give me wisdom about how to guide them. You might say I was like a mother to Israel.

People respected what I said, because they knew that God spoke through me.

It was a hard time for our country. Our enemies had chariots and weapons made of iron. We had no chariots and no such weapons. Our enemies controlled all the good, flat land. We had to flee to the hill country and the mountains where it was harder to grow crops.

One day God told me, "Enough of this! Call the warrior Barak. I am about to give you a great victory!"

Barak's Script

I am Barak. Some people call me one of the greatest warriors in all Israel. I think that's a joke. We have brave fighting men, but there's not much we can do when our enemies are all around us with chariots and better weapons!

One day Deborah called me and said, "This is what the Lord, the God of Israel commands you. Call 10,000 fighting men to meet our enemies at Mount Tabor. There I will give you victory over them."

I know 10,000 men sounds like a big army to you, but you have no idea what our enemies are like! They just run us down with their chariots. Their general is named Sisera. Everyone fears him. I didn't want to disobey Deborah, but I could hardly believe what she was ordering me to do!

Finally I answered, "I will go to battle, but only if you go with me."

Deborah would not fight, but she would be like the voice of God to our men. It has long been a custom in Israel for prophets to go with the army and tell them God's will. So Deborah went with us.

The armies of the Living God of Israel waited on the slopes of a great mountain. The armies of our enemy Sisera spread out with their chariots in the valley below.

Suddenly Deborah shouted, "Get ready! This is the day the Lord will give you victory over Sisera, for the Lord is marching ahead of you!"

At her words, our army roared down the mountain with fierce battle cries. The Lord God threw Sisera and all his chariots and warriors into a panic! Sisera saw they were losing, so he ran away on foot.

Published in *All Together Now, Volume 4* by Group Publishing, Inc., 1515 Cascade Ave., Loveland, CO 80538.

Jael's Script

I am Jael. My husband's people are distant relatives of the Israelites. We knew of the great battle between Sisera and the Israelites, but had no part in it. My husband was friendly with both Sisera's people and the Israelites, but of course our love was for the Israelites, our own relatives.

We knew that Sisera had been cruel to the Israelites for many years. Our hearts grieved for them, but being a small family, there was nothing we could do to help. Until the day of the battle, that is.

My husband was gone that day, and I was alone in my tent. Imagine my amazement when the great Sisera himself came staggering to our camp. He was worn out from battle. But still, he was a great warrior and I was a woman alone. How could I protect myself? I could not fight him, so I pretended to offer him shelter.

In my time, a woman was forbidden to offer shelter to a man when her husband was not home. Sisera knew it was not proper. I would not let him ruin my family name or hurt my relatives the Israelites anymore. So I, a mere housewife, took the life of the great general Sisera. In my time, there was no greater shame for a soldier than to die at the hands of a woman.

When Barak, the leader of God's army, came chasing Sisera, I showed him where the evil man lay, slain by my own hand. After that, our people lived in peace for 40 years.

Published in *All Together Now, Volume 4* by Group Publishing, Inc., 1515 Cascade Ave., Loveland, CO 80538.

Say: **This nifty little box is to remind you that ★** *God invites all kinds of people into his kingdom,* **and that includes you!**

The instructions for assembling the pyramid boxes are printed on the handout. Encourage kids to make their folds precise and crease them with a fingernail. When the folds are nicely creased, the pyramid boxes practically fall together. Help kids hole punch the circles, being careful not to puncture through the tips of the pyramid. Do not have them attach the ribbon just yet.

Have early finishers lend a hand to those who have not yet completed their projects and then help clean up the area.

Say: **Your boxes look terrific! But they seem to be missing something.**

Ask:

• **What do you think our boxes need?**

Say: **Right! They need people to work for God's kingdom! Let's see about adding some of those.**

COMMITMENT
....

Steppin' Up

Ask:

• **What kind of people does God invite into his kingdom?**

Say: **You've got it! ★** *God invites all kinds of people into his kingdom.*

Ask:

• **How about you? If God wants all kinds of people serving in his kingdom, how can** *you* **take part?**

For each way that kids think of, add a few gummy bears to their "All Kinds of People" boxes. Note that the bears come in different colors, just as people come with different possible ways to serve in God's kingdom.

Say: **I wonder if you've ever thought before that God might have you help make a difference in his kingdom. Really! God** *always* **calls on people who are tuned in to him, ready to do his will. Let's all eat a gummy bear and tell one way God might invite us into his kingdom.**

Hand each child a length of curling ribbon. Demonstrate how to double the ribbon and then slide the ribbon through two opposite holes in the top of the box. Then kids will lace the ribbon through the other two holes and gently tie the ribbon in a bow.

All Together Now

All Kinds of People

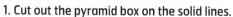

1. Cut out the pyramid box on the solid lines.
2. Fold back and crease on all the dotted lines.
3. Punch holes through the circles near the tips of the points.
4. Thread ribbon through the holes to tie the box shut.

GOD USES

ALL KINDS OF PEOPLE

DEBORAH THE JUDGE

BARAK THE WARRIOR

JAEL THE HOUSEWIFE

THE AMAZING YOU!

IN HIS KINGDOM!

JUST LIKE YOU

Published in *All Together Now, Volume 4* by Group Publishing, Inc., 1515 Cascade Ave., Loveland, CO 80538.

65

CLOSING

Bear Share

Say: **Please take your "All Kinds of People" boxes home and tell how each person helped in today's Bible passage, beginning with Deborah. Then untie the bows at the top of your box and invite each person in your family to tell how they might help in God's kingdom and then take a gummy bear. What a fun way to teach your family that ★** *God invites all kinds of people into his kingdom!*

All Together Now

A King's the Thing

You'll need...

- ☐ scissors
- ☐ glue sticks
- ☐ pens or pencils
- ☐ copies of the "Follow God!" handout (p. 75)

LESSON AIM

To help kids know that ★ *no matter what others do, God wants us to follow him.*

OBJECTIVES

Kids will

- ✓ obey instructions in conflicting ways,
- ✓ participate in a cue and response account about Saul, Israel's first king,
- ✓ explore the Bible point with the "Follow God!" booklet, and
- ✓ name ways they'll follow God this week.

BIBLE BASIS

 1 Samuel 8:1—13:14

A young man named Saul went out in search of his father's missing donkeys. Before he returned, he ran into the aging prophet Samuel, who proclaimed him Israel's first king. Wow, God *does* like to surprise us!

It had been a long time since Israel had a strong military leader. The Philistines were encroaching on their territory on one side, the Ammonites on the other. Still without the benefit of iron and bronze, the Israelites couldn't even sharpen their farming tools without going to their enemies and paying hefty prices. At one point the Philistines even stole the Ark of the Covenant! But it brought such great suffering upon whichever city had it that they sent it back to Israel of their own free will—along with offerings to the God of Israel.

The Israelites didn't connect their suffering as a nation to their continued disobedience of God. Instead they blamed their struggles on the lack of strong leadership. They went to the aging Samuel, Israel's last judge, and demanded a king—like all the other countries had.

From this perspective, the childishness of that demand seems obvious: *We want what everybody else has!*

In some ways it's amusing, in others, it's tragic. Throughout Israel's history, God had maintained a special relationship with that nation as Israel's heavenly sovereign. But it was very hard for God's people to follow the One they could not see. From the time they left Egypt and its visible false gods to this struggle with the false gods of the Canaanites, the Israelites willfully pulled toward the material world, away from the Holy One whose great miracles had formed them and saved them time after time throughout their long history. And now they were at it again, rejecting a special relationship with an unseen God in favor of an earthly king, flawed as he might be.

Saul himself was a conundrum. Though he was tall and handsome, he began with an appealing humility—*who me? I'm a nobody from the smallest tribe!* Later, when lots were cast with all the people present to choose a king and it fell to Saul, he was found hiding among the luggage. Then, once affirmed as king, Saul made no undue moves to throw his weight around. All good so far.

Sadly, this auspicious beginning quickly took a negative turn that struck a fatal blow to Saul's young monarchy. The Philistines posed a serious threat. Under Samuel's orders, Saul mounted an army at Gilgal and waited seven days for Samuel to join them and make the appropriate sacrifices before battle. Seeing the strength of the Philistines, Saul's army began to melt away in fear. On the seventh day, when Samuel still had not yet arrived, Saul feared the rest of his army might desert as well, so he took the matter of the sacrifice into his own hands. Only this was not kingly business—it was priestly business. Saul was only a military leader, *not* the intercessor between the people and God.

Just as Saul finished the inappropriate sacrifice, Samuel arrived, greatly aggrieved to see how quickly the new king had disobeyed God. The prophet announced that because of Saul's disobedience, his kingdom must end, and that God had already appointed another king to follow him, a man after God's own heart.

And so Saul becomes a tragic, tormented figure sandwiched

All Together Now

between Samuel and David. He's a king demanded by a disobedient people who preferred to be like other nations rather than follow their unique heritage as people attached solely to the living God.

📖 **Romans 12:1-2**

Presenting ourselves as a "living and holy sacrifice" and allowing God to change our thinking is tough—day in and day out. God has plans for us to be one way, but we live in a world that's another way. The world's way is all around us, constantly bombarding us. We have to *seek* God's way, *choose* it, become *disciples* of it. Unless we turn our faces to God daily, God's ways can slip through our fingers.

The people of God made a bold choice to turn away from his sovereignty in favor of earthly monarchs. We too make choices each day. Stop and think. Ask for God's transforming power. God loves to give it!

UNDERSTANDING YOUR KIDS

"But everybody else has one."
"But everybody else gets to watch that show."
"But all my friends are wearing those."
"But *why* can't I go?"

Kids may see nothing but limitations as we train them to make God-honoring choices. The truth is, being transformed into God's likeness is a process that begins with our first steps of faith and never ends. As God changes us, we reflect more and more of the perfect love in which we were created.

It's hard to turn our backs on the attractive things of the world and choose instead the holy things of God, whether it involves following an earthly king or choosing a modest outfit or a show that avoids sexual content. Use this lesson to teach your kids that choosing God's way is always the right thing to do.

THE LESSON »

ATTENTION GRABBER

Who You Gonna Follow?

Greet children warmly. As they arrive, casually assign them to two groups. Explain that you'll be depending on both groups to carry out your instructions, so you'll need to step outside the room for a moment of coaching with each of them.

Outside the room, say to Group 1:

I'm counting on you to be the leaders during this activity. Pay close attention and do exactly what I say. I know I can trust you to stick right with me, even if other kids mess up a little. Are you with me?

Give high fives to everyone in Group 1.

Then call Group 2 outside the room for their briefing.

Say: **I'm giving you a challenging job this morning! Your job is to mess up my instructions, but not too much. For instance, when I say to do 10 jumping jacks, do just 5 and then quit. When I tell you to touch your toes, touch the top of your head instead. When I say to hop on one foot, bounce on both feet. When I say to hop on the other foot, keep bouncing on both feet. Pretend like your hearing is just a little bit off, OK? If anyone tries to correct you, just keep doing what you're doing.**

Ask the kids in Group 2 to repeat your instructions, pass around high fives, and then return to the room.

Say: **We're all going to need a good warm-up for today's lesson. Let's form one big circle and get started.**

Let's start with 10 big jumping jacks. Count aloud with me.

Group 1 will stay with you; Group 2 will stop at five. Ignore the discrepancy and move on.

Say: **Good job! Now shake out a little, and then reach down and touch your toes.**

Group 1 will touch their toes; Group 2 will touch the tops of their heads. Again, ignore what's happening and go on.

Say: **Now for a little hopping fun. Pat your left leg. Now hop on your left foot.**

Group 1 will hop on their left feet; Group 2 will bounce on both feet.

Say: **Time to switch. Pat your right leg. Hop on your right foot.**

Teacher Tip

Leave an assistant or trusted, older child in charge when you step out of the room with each group.

Teacher Tip

As everyone forms a large circle, make sure kids from both groups are intermixed.

Again, Group 1 will hop on their right feet; Group 2 will bounce on both feet.

Say: **OK. Join me in a huddle and let's talk about what just happened.**

Ask:

• **What was it like when not everyone was following my instructions?**

• **Would you have rather followed my instructions or done something else—and why?**

Say: **You see, I asked Group 2 not to follow my instructions exactly. That created quite a bit of confusion. Today we're going to learn that ★ *no matter what others do, God wants us to follow him.* Just as with this experience, it can be hard to follow when people all around are doing whatever they please. Let's find out what happened when God's people, the Israelites, decided they wanted to do what everyone else was doing rather than following God.**

BIBLE EXPLORATION

We Want a King! (1 Samuel 8:1–13:14)

Have kids join you in a story circle.

Ask:

• **Describe what you think the expression "between a rock and a hard place" means.**

Say: **The Israelites found themselves *between a rock and a hard place* at the beginning of today's Bible passage. The rock on the one side was Philistia, the land of the Philistines. The hard place on the other side was Ammon, the land of the Ammonites. Let's see what that looks like. Groups 1 and 2, would you please stand up again?**

Choose a small child from one of the groups. Have that child stand in the middle of the groups. Direct the groups each to form a large clump that presses (not too hard!) around the child.

Put your hand on the head of the child in the middle and explain that he or she represents the land of Israel, squished between the more powerful nations of Philistia and Ammon.

Have the kids take their seats in the story circle again.

Say: ***That's* what I meant when I said that Israel was caught between a rock and a hard place. God only promised to keep blessing the Israelites if they obeyed him.**

Unfortunately, many of the Israelites disobeyed God by worshipping false gods—idols of wood or stone that they could see rather than the great God they couldn't see—the God who made all the heavens and the earth. And so God allowed these great enemies, the Philistines and the Ammonites, to make life hard for his people.

But did the Israelites stop to think, *this must be happening to us because we've disobeyed God?* No! That was the last thing on their minds! But before I tell you what they were thinking, I need to get you involved with the passage. I'm going to repeat a few important words as our passage continues. Each time I say one of these important words, you need to give a certain response. Let's take a moment to learn the cues and responses.

Practice these cues and responses with the kids. Each time you teach a response, model it and have kids do it with you.

- ✓ Whenever I say "Israelites," say, "the people of God."
- ✓ Whenever I say "enemies," make a terrible scary face.
- ✓ Whenever I say "the prophet Samuel," bow and say, "a man of God."
- ✓ Whenever I say "king," use your hands to make a crown on your head.
- ✓ Whenever I say "God," point to the sky and shout, "Almighty!"

Call out the cue words in random order to make sure the kids have the responses down. Rehearse until you're satisfied that the kids are confident with their responses.

In the passage below, each of the cue words is underlined for your convenience. Emphasize the cue words, pausing to let children respond with vigor.

Say: **The *Israelites* felt pressed in on all sides by their *enemies*. The always powerful Philistines lived on the coast of the Mediterranean Sea. They had chariots and weapons made of iron. The *Israelites* had no such weapons.**

Across the Jordan valley lived the Ammonites. They were cruel people who made terrible threats! I promise you this: You wouldn't want to have the Ammonites for *enemies!*

Together, the Philistines and the Ammonites made life hard for the *Israelites*. Finally the *Israelites* went to *the prophet Samuel* and said, "We want a *king*! After all, look

All Together Now

at all the strong nations around us. They have a *king*. Why shouldn't we?"

The prophet Samuel felt his heart break when he heard the people demanding a *king*. You see, the *Israelites* had always had a special relationship with *God*. They needed no earthly *king* because *God* himself ruled them, watched over them, and sent prophets and judges to guide them. But the people decided to turn away from *God*. They wanted to be like other nations and have an earthly leader instead. They didn't understand that ★ *no matter what others do,* God *wants us to follow him.* It was a sad day, but *God* decided to give the people what they wanted. And here's how it happened.

A young man named Saul set off on an errand to find his father's missing donkeys. On the way, he met *the prophet Samuel*. *God* told *the prophet Samuel,* "This is the one I have chosen to be *king*." So *the prophet Samuel* poured special oil on Saul's head and told him that he would be the first *king* of the *Israelites*.

Saul was tall and handsome, but this new job was a total surprise to him. He went home to his father and did nothing about it.

Finally, when Israel's *enemies* pressed for war, Saul called together an army for battle. *The prophet Samuel* told Saul to wait seven days. On the seventh day the prophet would come and make a special sacrifice before battle. But there was a problem. As Saul and his army waited, the Philistine army got closer and closer. When Saul's army saw how powerful the Philistines were, some of the *Israelites* began to run away.

Saul was afraid that if he waited for *the prophet Samuel,* his army would all run away, so instead of waiting, Saul made the sacrifice himself—not good. That was not a job for a *king*, it was a job for a priest! *The prophet Samuel* arrived just as the *king* finished making the sacrifice, and was the prophet ever angry! Already the new *king* had disobeyed *God*. He hadn't trusted that *God* could take care of the *Israelites'* enemies.

That was it for Saul. *The prophet Samuel* gave him the sad news that his reign would not last. In fact, *God* had already chosen someone else to be *king*—someone who loved and trusted *God* with all his heart.

Congratulate kids for their great work in helping tell the passage. Then ask:

• **Describe whether you'd rather have God or an earthly king for a ruler—and why.**

• **What did the Israelites learn about a king being able to solve their problems?**

• **How did King Saul show that his faith was not in God?**

Say: **The Israelites were supposed to be God's special people, but they chose to be like all the other nations. When we put our faith in Jesus, we become God's special children.**

Ask:

• **How do we sometimes choose not to act like God's special children, but like everyone around us?**

• **What's one way we can choose to act like God's special children?**

Say: ★*No matter what others do, God wants us to follow him.* **Let's see what that might look like in our lives this week.**

LIFE APPLICATION

Follow God!

Lead kids to your craft table.

Say: **Today we're going to put feet on our Bible point! Check this out.**

Hold up your folded sample "Follow God!" feet.

Say: **Ready to hit the road? Here we go! See the dotted lines in the middle of the feet? Fold the page carefully in half horizontally on those lines. Make a hard crease.**

Keeping the page folded, fold it in half the other way, again using the center lines. Now you're ready to cut out all four feet at once.

After kids have done their cutting, show them how to glue the blank sides of the feet together to form a four-page booklet joined at the bottom of the feet. Have them fold the booklet so that the page entitled *Times When It's Hard to Follow God* is on top.

Say: **Would you look at that! Now let's get deeper into understanding that ★***no matter what others do, God wants us to follow him.***

Prep Box

Prepare a "Follow God!" craft for kids to examine. Set out scissors, glue sticks, pens or pencils, and copies of the "Follow God!" handout (p. 75).

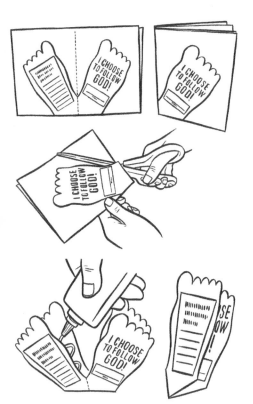

All Together Now

Follow God!

Don't copy the behavior and customs of this world, but let God transform you into a new person by changing the way you think. Then you will learn to know God's will for you.

ROMANS 12:2

I CHOOSE TO FOLLOW GOD!

SIGNED

Times When It's Hard to Follow God

Ways I'll Follow God This Week

Published in *All Together Now, Volume 4* by Group Publishing, Inc., 1515 Cascade Ave., Loveland, CO 80538.

COMMITMENT

. . . .

Follow God Moments

Lead kids through the booklet page by page, beginning with the page *Times When It's Hard to Follow God*. Let kids talk about times they're tempted to be like everyone else, the way the Israelites were when they wanted a king because all the other nations had one.

Move on to Romans 12:2. Have a willing child read it aloud. Invite kids to discuss how this can become a reality in their lives.

The page kids can sign is an opportunity for them to willingly take on this challenge. **Say ★ *No matter what others do, God wants us to follow him.* That's a big challenge for anyone. We need God's help and the support of our Christian brothers and sisters to do it. Are you ready for the challenge? Think about it before you sign this page. If you'd rather not sign the page right now, that's fine. That means you're taking this challenge seriously and want to give it more thought.**

On the last page, let kids brainstorm ways they'll follow God this week in potentially difficult situations.

Say: **Great thinking, everyone! I have confidence that you'll be great God-followers!**

CLOSING

. . . .

A Prayer for God-Followers

Have kids join you in a circle for your closing prayer.

Pray: **Dear God, we know that ★ *no matter what others do, you want us to follow you.* We want to follow you, but it's hard sometimes. Please change us from the inside out so we're more like you each day. In Jesus' name, amen.**

All Together Now

An Unlikely Choice for King

LESSON AIM

To help kids know ★ *God cares about what's in our hearts.*

OBJECTIVES

Kids will

✓ create food people,

✓ use their food people to participate in the telling about the choosing of David and slaying of Goliath,

✓ make a survey of David's heart and their own hearts, and

✓ commit to opening their hearts to God.

BIBLE BASIS

 1 Samuel 16:1—17:49

Saul, Israel's first king, turned out to be a miserable failure. He refused to follow God's instructions, made excuses, tried to weasel his way out of his infractions, and then tried to appease God by obeying too late. God informed Saul through Samuel that his future as Israel's king was all but over, that he would have no dynasty, and that in fact God had already chosen his replacement—a man after God's own heart. Tough words for a man in power to hear! And, as we'll see in the next few lessons, Saul didn't give up his throne easily.

God sent Samuel to Bethlehem to anoint the next king from Jesse's family. After meeting all of Jesse's older sons, Samuel wasn't satisfied and asked if there were any more sons. No one

You'll need...

- ☐ antiseptic hand cleanser
- ☐ foam cups
- ☐ food items kids can use to build people, such as marshmallows (mini and regular size), toothpicks, gumdrops, circus peanuts, marshmallow creme, and licorice twirls*
- ☐ recycled office paper
- ☐ permanent marker
- ☐ copies of the "A Heart Like David's?" handout (p. 86)
- ☐ scissors
- ☐ glue sticks
- ☐ markers

* Always check for allergies before serving snacks.

had even thought of bringing young David in from watching the sheep. (The next time you feel slighted, think of young David and remember that God makes things turn out as they should.)

Sure enough, the ruddy and handsome young David was the one God had in mind. For, as God informed the surprised Samuel, God looks past the outer shell and into a person's heart. It turns out that David's experience handling a wandering, stubborn flock was just what was needed to unite the stubborn, wandering people of Israel.

Samuel anointed David in the privacy of his family, this time using a special anointing horn (as described in the New International Version of the Bible) for the occasion and likely using the anointing oil specified in Exodus 30. Everyone present understood that Saul would remain king even though David was now God's chosen one. God's Spirit entered David—a full and constant entering, not given just for certain occasions—and left Saul. Saul then became dangerously despondent.

David stepped gloriously into the military picture via the well-known saga of his slaying of the Philistine giant, Goliath. The Philistines and the Israelites faced off at the valley of Elah. Each day, the 9-foot Goliath came out and taunted the Israelites to send out someone to face him in single combat. The nation of the loser would become slaves to the nation of the winner.

David, though he was already anointed king, accepted the humble task of staying home to tend his father's sheep while his older brothers went to war. While delivering food to his brothers, he was affronted by the Philistine's taunts against the God of Israel. Here's where we see what God saw in David: He cared nothing for the difference in size and armaments. What David saw was God being insulted, and he had ultimate faith in God's power.

While a sling may seem like a child's toy to us, it had long been used as a weapon. In the hands of a skilled slinger, its long-range accuracy could be deadly—as we see in this passage.

David's popularity soars following his defeat of the Philistine hero giant, resulting in Saul's growing jealousy and mistrust of the future king. We see Saul gradually descend into madness and, ultimately, self-destruction. God was with one and had left the other. May we always be with God in all that we do!

 **Mark 12:30**

Young David's defeat of Goliath came not from zeal to be a mighty warrior, nor to gain fame on the field of battle, but because

All Together Now

he held the name of God to be holy and could not stand to hear it mocked. This passion for God guided David throughout his life. It wasn't a life without fault. But David was a person God chose to bless, someone who knew how to pray to God in psalms that thousands of years later still express the feelings in our hearts. David was a person whose deep humility before God led to the only divinely appointed dynasty, which itself led to the birth of the Messiah.

When asked a trick question by the Pharisees, Jesus quickly solved this mystery of why some were blessed while others were cast away: "And you must love the Lord your God with all your heart, all your soul, all your mind, and all your strength." God loves those who love *him* with all their heart, soul, mind, and strength.

When our human nature collides with Jesus' divine love, Jesus transforms us into people who carry that passionate love of God. We live and work not for our own glory, but for the glory that will come to the God we love.

UNDERSTANDING YOUR KIDS

There's a humble spirit about David, his lack of need to be recognized, that doesn't come naturally to most kids. That humility requires a certain grace that comes with maturity.

What kids *can* emulate is David's steady confidence in God. Somehow David failed to fear what others feared. He must have had an intimate knowledge of God's greatness to step up to single combat with a bully of Goliath's proportions. But who was Goliath compared to the living God?

Having this kind of confidence in the maker and master of the universe is one of our greatest challenges. In choosing David, God didn't see the tallest, most impressive man. He saw a young person of unshakable faith and humble heart who yearned for intimacy with his maker—the Lord God of Israel. These are attributes our kids can embrace.

Use this lesson to teach kids that God values a true and faithful heart above all else.

THE LESSON »

ATTENTION GRABBER

Food People

Greet kids warmly, and have them wipe their hands with an antiseptic cleanser.

Say: **Here's your opening challenge. It's a fun one! Use any of the materials you see to build a person. Turn your foam cup over and use it for the base of your person. For instance, if you'd like to use toothpicks for legs, you can stick them into your foam cup to make your person sit. Or you can smear marshmallow creme on the base of the cup to stick on whatever you choose for legs. With the cups as bases, we can move our people around without damaging them.**

The goal is for you to keep your creation secret. Don't look at anyone else's person as you build. Fold a sheet of paper in half to build a shield around your person so no one can see what you're building. Be as creative as you like. Your person can be very short or very tall, narrow or wide, crazy-looking or realistic. It's up to you.

There's no race or contest either. Eventually we'll use all our people in today's Bible passage. I'll give you about five minutes to build your people, so get going!

Give kids a one-minute warning, and then call time. Have kids pull away their paper shields and show the "people" they've built. Let kids walk around the work area to admire each other's food people.

Thank kids for their effort in making their creations.

Encourage kids to comment on their favorite things about each other's creations.

As kids return to their seats, say: **When we look at people, we often look at them just like we looked at these interesting food people. We notice things about the way they look and we judge what we like about their appearance. But guess what? God sees people differently.** ★ *God cares about what's in our hearts.* **Let's see how that plays out in today's Bible passage.**

All Together Now

BIBLE EXPLORATION

More Than a Shepherd Boy (1 Samuel 16:1–17:49)

Have kids line up their food people in a row.

Say: **I'll tell you about the people we'll need for our Bible passage, and then you can decide which food person we'll use for each person.**

We'll need a giant, a tall king, an older prophet, a father, some older brothers, and a young shepherd boy.

Give kids time to decide how to "cast" the Bible passage using the food people they've made. When the people are chosen, write the following names on the supporting foam cups: Goliath, King Saul, Prophet Samuel, Jesse, Jesse's Sons (as many as you have), David.

Say: **As I tell what happened, it'll be your job to move your people around on the table at the appropriate times.** As you retell this story, pause often to allow kids to move around their cup people. You can either read the story that follows on pages 82 to 84 or retell it in your own words based on this account.

David's Heart for God

God told the Prophet Samuel to travel to a little town called Bethlehem. Why is Bethlehem famous?

Bethlehem is also famous because the main person we're talking about today is Jesus' greatest ancestor. So listen carefully and see if you can figure out who it is.

In Bethlehem, Samuel was to visit a man named Jesse. God would show Samuel which one of Jesse's sons would be the next king of Israel. God told Samuel to take a horn filled with special oil. When God showed Samuel the next king, Samuel would pour this special oil from the horn onto his head. To be anointed this way was truly a great honor.

When Samuel and Jesse met, Samuel asked to meet all of Jesse's sons. Samuel wondered which one of these sons God would choose for the next king of Israel. So all of Jesse's sons stood before Samuel. The oldest one looked tall and handsome. Samuel wondered if God would choose the oldest son to be king, but God said no. You see, Samuel looked on the outside, but ★ *God cares about what's in our hearts.* God said no to the other sons, too.

Samuel asked Jesse, "Do you have any other sons?"

Jesse was surprised at Samuel's question. Didn't he already have his strongest, handsomest sons standing before the prophet? But he answered truthfully.

"My youngest son is out watching the sheep."

Watching the sheep was the *least* important job of all. There wasn't much glory in being a shepherd, so it was no surprise that Jesse had given this job to his youngest son.

But Samuel said, "We will not sit down to dinner until he arrives."

Hmm. I bet the older brothers grumbled to each other about that.

When the young shepherd David arrived, God told Samuel, "This is the one! This is the next king of Israel!"

Samuel could see that David looked tan and strong from his days spent outdoors looking after his father's sheep. Samuel took the special horn filled with oil and spilled the oil over David's head, announcing to Jesse and his family that David was God's choice for the next king of Israel.

Jesse's older sons probably grumbled again. After all, older brothers tend to think they're a lot stronger and wiser than younger brothers, don't they?

They may have grumbled all right, but Samuel was God's high priest. Everyone knew that God spoke through Samuel. So if Samuel said David was to be the next king, then David was to be the next king and that was that.

After Samuel left, David went right back to caring for his father's sheep, just as he had done before. You see, Saul was still the ruling king. David was to be the *next* king when the time came for a new king. In the meantime, it didn't bother David to obey his father and live as humbly as he had before.

Ask:

• **Describe how you'd feel about doing your chores and obeying your parents if you knew you'd someday be king.**

Not long after that, Jesse's older sons went off to war. King Saul and the Israelite army lined up on a hill overlooking one side of a long valley. The enemy Philistines lined up on the hill on the opposite side of the valley. The Philistines had a champion, a giant named Goliath. I'll bet you've never seen anyone as tall as Goliath. He was over 9 feet tall—taller than any basketball player!

Every day Goliath came down from the hill and made fun of the Israelites and their God. He challenged anyone to come out and fight him man to man. But all the Israelites were scared of the giant. He wore armor made of bronze from head to toe. No sword or spear could pierce it. He towered over even the tallest soldier. How could anyone fight the giant and win? Rather than sending anyone out to fight, the Israelites trembled in their tents when the giant called out and made fun of God.

That is, until one day when David came to the Israelite camp bringing food to his older brothers. He heard the Philistine giant calling out insults to the God of Israel. David couldn't believe it! Who would *dare* insult God?

Although David was just a teenager, he went to King Saul and volunteered to fight the giant. King Saul wondered how a young boy could defeat a giant. David explained that while he watched over his sheep in the wilderness, he had fought off both lions and bears. He believed that the God who helped him defeat lions and bears would also help him defeat Goliath.

Saul put his own armor on David, but it was way too big. David felt clumsy in the heavy armor. He was a shepherd, not a soldier. He was used to running free, not wearing heavy armor. So David took off Saul's armor and went to fight the Philistine his own way, wearing just his tunic and armed with a simple shepherd's sling.

A sling was one long piece of rope or leather with a loop at both ends and a wide section in the middle to hold a stone. A good slinger could whirl it and then let go of one end, sending the stone sailing at high speed toward its target. Good slingers had worked as soldiers for many centuries. A stone or other small object slung at high speed could fly a long distance with deadly accuracy. But the giant Goliath had no respect for David's skill with a sling.

Goliath laughed when he saw the small shepherd who had come to fight him. He asked, "You come at me with sticks and stones?"

David answered confidently, "I come in the name of the living God!"

David had no fear of Goliath's size at all. He knew that God was much, much bigger than any man—no matter how big. So he put a smooth stone into his sling, whirled it around and around, and then with great skill let it go at just the right time. Smack! The stone hit the giant right in the forehead and down he fell.

The Israelites all praised David and made him a great hero, but David knew that the victory was God's. David had kept his heart open to God, and something amazing happened.

Have kids give themselves and their food people a round of applause for their participation during the passage. Then let kids eat their food people as you discuss:

• **If you were choosing someone to be king, what kind of person would you choose—and why?**

• **What do you think made David different from everyone else when it came to standing up to the giant?**

• **Why do you think David would make a good king?**

• **Why do you think God cares more about what's in a person's heart than what we see on the outside?**

LIFE APPLICATION
. . . .

A Heart Like David's?

Prep Box

Prepare a sample "A Heart Like David's?" craft for kids to see. Set out scissors, glue sticks, and copies of the "A Heart Like David's?" handout (p. 86).

Lead kids to the craft area.

Say: **Learning about David helps us see that ★ *God cares about what's in our hearts.* This craft will give us a good opportunity to look into David's heart—and then into yours!**

Instructions for cutting and folding the heart are printed on the handout. After kids have cut out and folded the handout, invite them to look carefully at what God found in David's heart. Let kids evaluate themselves. If they feel God would find those same characteristics in their hearts, invite them to draw an arrow from each characteristic to the left panel that reads, "Good Things In My Heart." Encourage older kids to help younger kids if they need it.

Say: **When we belong to Jesus, he's always growing good things in our hearts, because day by day he makes us more and more like him.**

COMMITMENT
. . . .

God at Work

Say: **No matter how hard we try, by ourselves we can't make our hearts better inside. That's God's work! What we *can* do is open our hearts to God and ask for help, because ★ *God cares about what's in our hearts.***

Explain to kids that you'll take a few moments for kids to open their hearts to God. Tell them that perhaps he'll show them ways

A Heart Like David's?

God liked what he saw in David's heart, so God chose him to be the next king of Israel. Look at what was in David's heart—would God find those same things in your heart?

Cut out the large piece on the solid lines, and fold the half-hearts inward to the middle. Cut out the rectangular tab, and glue half of it to the left heart-half. Make sure the other half of the tab extends over the right heart half.

Go over David's characteristics. How can you make them part of your life?

GOD FOUND SPECIAL THINGS IN DAVID'S HEART. WILL HE FIND THEM IN YOUR HEART?

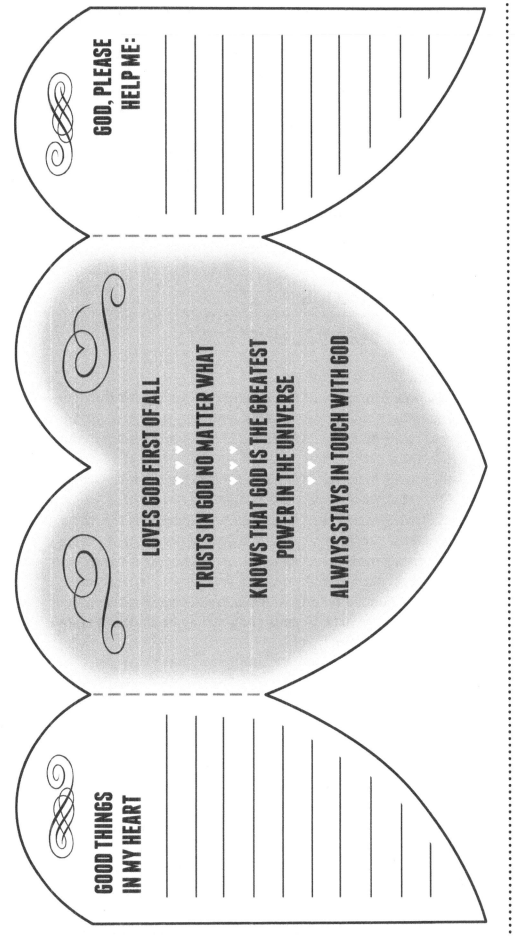

GOD, PLEASE HELP ME:

LOVES GOD FIRST OF ALL

TRUSTS IN GOD NO MATTER WHAT

KNOWS THAT GOD IS THE GREATEST POWER IN THE UNIVERSE

ALWAYS STAYS IN TOUCH WITH GOD

GOOD THINGS IN MY HEART

he'd like to help them grow good things in their hearts. Assure kids that if they don't hear anything in their time of quiet prayer, that's OK too. They can take their hearts home and use them during prayer time all week.

Say: **I'll open with prayer; then let's all be quiet for a few seconds as we ask God to speak to us. Then I'll close our prayer time.**

Pray: **Dear God, we know you care about what's in our hearts. We want to have hearts like David—hearts that please you. We quiet ourselves before you now and invite you to show us ways you can grow good things in our hearts.**

Hold silence for as long as 30 seconds. Then say: **In Jesus' name we pray, amen.**

Ask the group if anyone would like to share ideas God gave them. There may be some "copycat" ideas and that's fine. It's good to get kids talking.

Invite kids to write their ideas on the right sides of their hearts. Have older kids assist younger ones who may need help with writing.

CLOSING
. . . .

Hearts Forward!

Have kids gather in a circle holding their heart handouts in front of their hearts.

Say: **People look on the outside, but** ★ *God cares about what's in our hearts.*

Have kids open their heart handouts.

Say: **Let's open our hearts to God this week and see what amazing things happen!**

David Runs for His Life

LESSON AIM

To help kids see that ★ *God helps us show mercy.*

OBJECTIVES

Kids will

✓ play a game of Slimy Keep Away,

✓ participate in an interactive story as David's mighty warriors,

✓ create a stand-up owl with a Bible verse on mercy, and

✓ plan a way to show mercy this week.

BIBLE BASIS

 1 Samuel 24

Mercy to a man caught in a downward spiral of hatred. Mercy without bounds. Mercy beyond reason.

Mercy to King Saul, now sinking ever deeper into evil insanity, was what the future King David proved again and again to possess in an almost incomprehensible degree. Years of David's life and the lives of his men were consumed in running from the king whom God had deserted. They lived in desperate conditions, subject to betrayal at any moment. Yet this was the life that David chose. God gave him the opportunity to change things by putting Saul's life in his hands on at least two occasions, one of which we'll look at today. On each of these occasions David chose mercy over self-preservation, much to the wonder and frustration of his followers.

You'll need...

- ☐ two pitchers of warm water
- ☐ bar of soap
- ☐ roll of paper towels
- ☐ small backpack
- ☐ dried fruit snack mix*
- ☐ small piece of fabric (to represent what David cut from Saul's tunic)
- ☐ copies of the "Full of Mercy" handout (p. 96)
- ☐ scissors
- ☐ cellophane tape
- ☐ optional: colored pencils

* Always check for allergies before serving snacks.

Is this merciful behavior of David's giving us a little glimpse of God's merciful attitude toward all of humankind? Of Jesus' submission to those who humiliated him and put him to death? For, if anything, David was a mighty warrior, a general who could lead his men with such fury that his enemies would simply melt away in fear.

Yet, rather than dispatching Saul, or allowing his men to do so, David moved his family to the country of Moab for safety, played the fool in the court of the Philistines, pretended to shift his loyalty, and lived for years as a hunted fugitive, barely surviving off the land and from the help of friendly locals who gave what they could to support him and his 600 mighty men. Why, we are compelled to ask, did he do so when simply dispatching the evil Saul would have been so much easier?

David's own answer is that he would do nothing to harm the Lord's anointed, even though he, too, was the Lord's anointed and the Spirit of God had long since left Saul.

Clearly, it was God who gave David such a tender heart toward his persecutor. As noted throughout the Old and New Testaments, mercy is highly treasured by God. It is a characteristic of God himself. Yet, though we have all received God's mercy, it can be difficult for us to pass it on to others. It's all too easy to slam shut the doors of mercy.

I confess to wanting to reason with David here. "Hey, Dave, what good is Saul doing for Israel, huh? He's certainly not leading the people toward God. He's insane, Dave—have you noticed? So you don't want to do the deed, I get that. But why not leave him to your men and get on with leading the kingdom as God has planned?"

That's what works on my level. Obviously I still have a lot of growing in grace to do. How about you?

 **James 3:17**

Don't you wish that wisdom from above came in a nice squirt bottle like soothing hand lotion does? For me it's always been a bit of a conundrum to understand this Saul-sparing David. This great warrior David would fight Israel's enemies on all sides and make the nation secure for the first time, but had such a tender conscience before God that he could not lay a finger on the mad king who for years made David's assassination his sole ambition.

Perhaps it was this very aspect of mercy that caused David to stand out in God's eyes. God calls David a man after his own heart.

All Together Now

Not a flawless person, mind you, but a person whose heart desired what God desired. May the same be said of us.

UNDERSTANDING YOUR KIDS

It's hard to teach kids to show mercy when ours is such a harsh world. Today as I write, the news has been dominated by a home-made video of a bullied child who chose to die at her own hand, and of the close of a several-day search for a missing fourth-grader with the discovery of her body. Grim reality indeed.

But *what if* the bullied child had met a few merciful children to encourage her in the midst of her sad journey? And *what if* the person who took an innocent life had been given wise and merciful guidance at critical junctures in his maturation experience? Would he have chosen to become someone else?

These hypothetical questions have little to bring to families suffering terrible loss. But they do highlight the need for people of mercy in a sadly fallen world.

So how do we teach kids the importance of showing mercy in their young lives? Some children seem to be born with a natural sense of kindness—a heart that reaches out to others. Others seem to be born to look out for their own interests. Still others may be more combative in their approach to life.

Being identified as a kind child can bring challenges of its own. Teachers may develop a habit of pairing such a child with kids who won't otherwise find a partner. Given years of maturity, we can understand this as an opportunity to show mercy. At the time, how-ever, the kind child may find him- or herself vicariously feeling like an outsider as well. We must emphasize that *every time* we show mercy and kindness to someone who might seem undeserving, we're reflecting the love of God himself.

We can model mercy in the way we handle our kids. We can quietly praise children who show mercy. If a disagreement arises, we can discuss and encourage merciful responses.

Use this lesson to help kids see the importance of showing mercy in all areas of their lives.

THE LESSON »

Prep Box

Outdoors is the best place for this activity, as the game will splash a small amount of soapy water. If you play inside, choose an area with an uncarpeted floor that kids can wipe up easily. Fill two large pitchers or other containers with warm water. Place a bar of soap in one of the pitchers.

Teacher Tip

You can play this game with nearly any small, slippery object. Soap works better than oil to make objects slippery, and it won't leave stains on clothes.

ATTENTION GRABBER

. . . .

Slimy Keep Away

As children arrive, greet them warmly and help them form two groups. Make sure each group has an equal number of taller children.

Say: **Today we're going to learn that ★** *God helps us show mercy.* **We'll begin by playing a super-fun game of Slimy Keep Away. And I've got a special place to play it. Follow me!**

Lead the kids to the play area. Have Group 1 kids form a circle and Group 2 kids stand in the center of the circle.

Say: **Here's how we play. Group 1 begins with this slippery bar of soap. Their job is to toss the soap to another team member on the opposite side of the circle. Group 2's job is to try to grab the soap while it's in the air. So to begin, it's Group 1's job to Keep Away and Group 2's job to snatch the soap. After someone in Group 2 has snatched the soap two times, your teams will trade places. Group 2 will form the circle and Group 1 will be the snatchers.**

Explain that kids will need to dip the soap in a pitcher every couple of throws to keep it nice and slippery. Keep paper towels nearby.

Let kids enjoy a few rounds of this rowdy game. If you play inside, have them use paper towels and work together to wipe the floor clean and dry. Then lead kids back to your room and have them sit in a discussion circle.

Ask:
• **What was fun about that game?**
• **What would make it even more fun?**

Say: **Now imagine what it would be like if you were trying to play Keep Away with a mad king who was trying to hunt you down. That's what happened to David in today's Bible passage. Let's find out if he was slippery enough to keep from being snatched by King Saul!**

BIBLE EXPLORATION

. . . .

David on the Run (1 Samuel 24)

Say: **David did a great thing and a terrible thing. The great thing was that he killed the enemy giant Goliath. And the terrible thing was that he killed the enemy giant Goliath.**

All Together Now

He also won many other battles. When he marched into town, the crowds shouted, "Saul has killed his thousands, but David has killed his tens of thousands." Hearing those shouts made King Saul jealous of young David. It didn't take long at all for that jealousy to grow to hatred and for the hatred to grow into plans to kill David.

David couldn't hang around the palace any more. He had to run and run fast. Immediately his brothers and other friends joined him. Soon he had a band of 600 mighty men who traveled with him. They were like the circle group in the Keep Away game. The group in the middle was like Saul's army. The mighty men kept hiding David while Saul and his army kept hoping they'd snatch him. Things went on this way for years and years.

You see, the Spirit of God had left King Saul and Saul became a mad man. No matter what happened to his nation, all he could think about was killing David. On the other hand, the Spirit of God was with David all the time. So even though he and his men lived a hard life running here and there, never having much to eat and always being hunted, they trusted God to be with them, provide for their needs and keep them safe.

Have kids stand. Explain that you are David and you will assess each of them to be one of his mighty men. Have kids touch both fingers to their nose, show you their muscles, or stand on one leg. Check kids' teeth, wiggle their noses. Make sure all your "inspections" are humorous and be careful not to point out anyone's faults.

Declare that all the children have passed inspection and can be part of David's band. Explain that you're going to be David and they will follow you closely.

Say: **One of our spies has brought word that Saul and his army are near, so we have to move from this place and find a place that's safer. There's a lot of danger out there, so stay as close to me as you can. Even a flash of bright clothing could give away our location!**

I know of a cave not too far from here. If we can get there without being seen, we'll be safe there. The cave is deep, so even if Saul and his men should stumble upon it, we can hide so deep inside it that they'll never see us at all.

Let's go for the cave! Are you with me?

Put on your backpack. Do a pile of hands for encouragement before you sneak out of the room together. Lead kids on a circuitous route through the church, inside and out, toward the destination you've chosen as your "cave." As you lead them, hug the walls, and peek around each corner before you motion the kids to follow you. Make the trip an adventure. Plan to have everyone a little out of breath when you arrive at your preplanned destination.

Pass around the snack mix and invite your brave warriors to enjoy some. Congratulate them on arriving safely without being seen by the enemy. Then suddenly look watchful and say: **Shh! Did you hear that?** Motion everyone to get down and be quiet.

Whisper: **I think I heard someone in the front of the cave. Look—it's King Saul himself! He must have come in here to rest. What's that? Oh...some of my other mighty men think that God has put Saul into my hands so I can kill him or so one of them can kill him.**

Ask:

• **Discuss whether you think I should kill King Saul. He's been trying to kill me for years. And God has already had me anointed as the next king.**

Let kids discuss your options in whispers.

Say: **My knife is here in my backpack.**

Secretly remove the piece of cloth from your backpack. Then move away from your kids, out of their sight, and then return, out of breath. Hold up the piece of cloth.

Say: **I could never kill my king, no matter how badly he treats me. He, too, is God's anointed. But I did cut this piece of cloth from the tunic he was wearing. He's left the cave now. Come with me—I'm going to call out to him.**

Lead the kids to the exit of your cave. Call out:

My lord, the king! Look at what I have in my hand. It is a piece of your robe! See, I'm not trying to harm you, even though you're hunting me. Don't listen to people who say I am trying to harm you!

Turn back to the kids and say: **I wonder how King Saul responded when he found out David had been *that* close to him but had shown mercy instead of killing him. Let's hurry back to our room to find out!**

Lead kids on a straight route back to your meeting room. Ask a volunteer to read aloud 1 Samuel 24:16-19 from an easy-to-understand version of the Bible.

Ask:

• **Suppose you were in King Saul's shoes and you discovered that David had just spared your life. How would you react?**

• **Tell why you think David could let Saul go free after Saul had been hunting him and trying to kill him for years.**

All Together Now

Say: **It was pretty amazing that David let Saul go. David showed a quality that is unusual in great warriors: He showed God's mercy. From the time David was a young shepherd boy alone in the fields for days at a time with the sheep, he'd had a close relationship with God. Because David spent a lot of time in God's presence, God gave David a merciful heart.**

David set a wonderful example for his men that day, and to all of us who have read this passage ever since. When we truly love God, we don't care about getting back at our enemies. We care much more about responding to them the way God does to us. When we live in close touch with God, ★ *God helps us show mercy*, just as he helped David show mercy to Saul.

LIFE APPLICATION

Full of Mercy

Lead kids to a craft table. Show your completed stand-up owl and say: **This wise old owl has some great advice for you. He'd like to stand by you to help you remember something important from God's Word. Let's get right to work on your very own wise owls.**

If you wish, let kids decorate the owl with colored pencils. Have kids cut out the owl and its stand in one piece and then cut open the slits on the stand. As kids work, ask a child volunteer to read the verse printed on the owl's wings aloud.

Ask:

• **What part of this verse reminds you of today's Bible passage?**

• **Tell whether you think God gave David the wisdom to be merciful to Saul.**

• **If someone's been mean to you, explain whether you think it feels better to get back at that person or to show mercy to that person.**

Say: **I know this: ★ *God helps us show mercy*. It's tough to do it on our own. If we lived without God's love, we might look for ways to get people back. Only a person who walks closely with God is wise enough to show mercy.**

Help kids slip the tabs of the handout base together to make it stand. Reinforce the connection with cellophane tape.

Prep Box

Prepare a sample "Full of Mercy" owl for kids to see. Set out scissors, cellophane tape, copies of the "Full of Mercy" handout (p. 96), and, if you wish, colored pencils.

Full of Mercy

God gave David special wisdom about what to do when Saul fell into David's hands. Instead of taking revenge, David showed mercy.

Read the wings of this wise old owl to find out where that kind of mercy comes from.

Keep this reminder about God's wisdom and mercy standing beside you!

Color in the owl and the base with colored pencils.

Cut out the owl and its stand all in one piece. Fold the wings on the dotted lines. Cut the slits on the base and hook them together to make the owl stand. Add tape to make the fastening secure.

It is full of mercy and good deeds. It shows no favoritism and is always sincere. JAMES 3:17

But the wisdom from above is first of all pure. It is also peace-loving, gentle at all times, and willing to yield to others.

96

COMMITMENT

Merciful Me?

Gather kids in a discussion circle with their owls.

Say: **David showed mercy to someone who made life difficult and dangerous for him and for his entire family! It's one thing to show mercy to someone who picks on you, but if that person makes life miserable and scary for your whole family, that's a different story, isn't it?**

Ask:

• **Describe how you feel when someone in your family gets picked on.**

Say: **David had to move his family to another country so they'd be safe. They had to leave their family's land behind. For the Israelites, a family's land was very important. It was part of their inheritance from God.**

It seems that Saul had hurt David in just about every way he could, yet David still showed mercy.

Ask:

• **Think silently about someone who makes your life hard or who's just irritating or sometimes mean.**

• **Now I'm going to ask a really hard question. How could you show mercy to that person this week?**

Say: **You don't have to answer out loud. It can be something just between you and God, because ★ *God helps us show mercy.* When you and God have a plan, set your owl on the floor in front of you. When all the owls are sitting on the floor, we'll close in prayer.**

Allow a minute for kids to process this question and what merciful action they'll take.

CLOSING

Forward in Mercy

Pray: **Dear God, we pray that you'll help us be merciful to others the way you're merciful to us. Thank you for ★ *helping us show mercy this week.* In Jesus' name we pray, amen.**

Abigail Saves the Day

LESSON AIM

To help kids know that ★ *God sends wise people into our lives to guide us.*

OBJECTIVES

Kids will

✓ play a game of Follow the Who?,

✓ hear from Lady Abigail about how she met David,

✓ make thank-you notes to share with wise people who've guided them, and

✓ commit to following wise spiritual leaders.

BIBLE BASIS

 1 Samuel 25:2-42

This account of David and Abigail gives us everything—the foolish, repulsive rich man, the angry warrior-prince, a bit of suspense, a wise woman hastening to make amends for her boorish husband, and finally, a touch of romance. We have here many of the archetypes of great storytelling, and your kids are going to love it.

David and his hungry men mingled among the shepherds of the rich Nabal during the annual sheepshearing, a time of great feasting and celebration in Israel. It was also a time when marauders could easily swoop in and steal a year's worth of profits from the owner of the sheep. In this case, David's men struck up a good rapport with the shepherds and guarded them.

You'll need...

- ☐ volunteer to play Abigail
- ☐ Bible-times costume with colorful scarves and gold or silver bracelets
- ☐ copy of "Abigail's Script" (pp. 104-106)
- ☐ beautiful cloth to cover Lady Abigail's chair
- ☐ copies of the "Bouquet of Thanks Card" handout (p. 108)
- ☐ scissors
- ☐ colored pencils
- ☐ glue sticks
- ☐ optional: 4x5-inch envelopes

Knowing that celebration would ensue in Nabal's household, David sent young men as messengers to Nabal with friendly greetings, information about how David's company had provided protection for the shearers, and a polite request for food.

Nabal, whose name means *fool* or *boorish,* responded in the most insulting way, calling David and his company runaway servants and implying that David himself was nobody. In a warrior culture, this kind of insult called for an immediate response—and David was God's anointed, thus Nabal had not only insulted David but God himself.

David immediately ordered his men to strap on their swords and prepare to march on the wealthy Nabal's home, swearing that no male of that household would survive.

Enter the brilliant and beautiful Abigail. One of Nabal's servants got word to her of her husband's foolish insolence toward David. Abigail knew of David's great service to the shepherds and probably feared he was preparing to march against her home. Wasting no time, Abigail prepared a generous food offering for David and his men, loaded it on donkeys and had the donkeys and servants precede her so that she intercepted David.

Upon meeting David, she bowed before him, as one would when addressing a king. She then addressed him as "my lord" ("adonai") and called herself a lowly servant even though she was a wealthy and influential woman. She delivered a brilliant speech to the affronted king-to-be. Abigail encouraged David not to sully his coming reign with needless bloodshed. She even prophesied that he would be the founder of a dynasty.

David was totally taken in by her gifts, her wisdom, and her beauty. He praised God for sending her to stop him from needlessly spilling blood.

Abigail didn't tell her boorish husband of her actions that night because he was rolling drunk. The next morning she did, however. Nabal's heart froze because he realized how close had been his brush with death. He suffered a stroke and died 10 days later.

On hearing of Nabal's death, David sent messengers asking Abigail to become his wife. Once again she acted quickly, gathering her five maidservants and belongings. The wise and beautiful Abigail married her handsome prince and all her wealth became David's. Now that's an amazing story!

Rabbinic tradition makes Abigail one of the most remarkable women in Jewish history. Her actions may well have turned the course of history, calling out the nobility in David rather than allowing vengeful bloodletting to stain his reputation.

All Together Now

📖 **Hebrews 13:17**

God graciously provides wise people to intervene in our lives at important times—*if* we're attuned to God's guidance and listening to the Holy Spirit. Mentors may appear in the way of friends who will come alongside us and speak into our lives for years. Or someone may drop a bit of wisdom on social media that is just the thing we need to hear. In the case of David and Abigail, God sent Abigail like a giant flashing red light on the freeway. *Stop, David! Think about what you're about to do!*

And the mighty warrior prince humbled himself and listened—to a *woman!* It was certainly not the norm in ancient Israel for a man of power to listen to a woman.

Therein lies a great lesson for us. Be on the lookout for wisdom when God puts it in our path. Be humble and ready to receive that which rings true with God's Word.

UNDERSTANDING YOUR KIDS

I'll confess, with the spiritual frauds we've seen in the headlines, with those who would take advantage of children, it's harder for me to write about entrusting kids to wise spiritual leaders than it used to be.

Our current church does a thorough background check on each person who wishes to be part of children's ministry. If yours doesn't, introduce the idea to your church leadership. Children's ministry is truly an area where we need to follow Jesus' advice about being as shrewd as snakes and harmless as doves (Matthew 10:16).

Review your guidelines for safe care of children from sign-in to sign-out, for visitors who want to have a look at your children's ministry, and for what to do in case of emergency. All this is not to be paranoid, but to be practical.

And now to the glorious, overarching truth of this lesson: God *will* send spiritual leaders into the lives of your kids at just the right time and place. Much of this will happen at church, some beyond its walls.

I've been especially grateful for the spiritual leaders God has sent into my own children's lives during their sensitive teenage years, during college years and military service, during courtship, and now young parenthood. At just the needed moment, someone always appeared through God's gracious providence to offer a nudge in the right direction. Seeing that pattern emboldens me to believe the same will happen for the beloved children in your spiritual care.

THE LESSON »

ATTENTION GRABBER

Follow the Who?

Give kids a warm welcome, and tell them you hope they're up for a challenging game.

Have everyone form a large circle. Ask for one brave child volunteer to leave the room for a moment. That person will be the Guesser.

Have the remaining kids decide who'll be the Leader. The Leader will initiate a motion for everyone to follow, such as clapping hands, marching in place, swinging arms, hopping on one foot, tapping heads, touching noses, or whatever creative idea kids come up with. Throughout the game, the Leader will change motions. The rest of the kids will follow what the Leader is doing.

Here's how to play. The Guesser comes back into the room and stands in the middle of the circle while the kids in the circle are already doing the first motion. At some point the Leader changes the motion and all the kids in the circle begin doing the new motion. After a few seconds, the Leader changes the motion again and the rest of the kids follow suit. The Guesser's job is to figure out which person in the circle is the Leader. The kids in the circle will try to keep the Leader's identity secret by not making eye contact or looking at the Leader too long.

Give the Guesser two chances to guess the Leader. Whether the Guesser guesses correctly or not, send the Leader outside the room to become the next Guesser. Choose a new Leader and continue the game for about 10 minutes.

After the game, invite everyone to sit.

Ask:

• **Describe what you think was fun about being the Leader.**

• **Tell what it was like to be the Guesser.**

• **Explain why you'd rather be a Leader or a Guesser.**

Say: **Sometimes life can leave us guessing! Should we do what we feel like doing, even though it might be a little wrong? Should we follow what others are doing? Or should we try to find a strong leader who might help us figure out what to do?**

If you've ever been confused about what to do, wave your hand at me.

Wave your hand at the kids to indicate that you, too, have felt confused about what to do.

All Together Now

Say: **It's good to know that** ★ *God sends wise people into our lives to guide us.* **Once this happened to me.**

Tell about a time God sent a wise person into your life to help you make an important decision.

Say: **Today we're going to learn that even David, the future king of Israel, needed guidance from a wise person to keep him from making a terrible mistake.**

BIBLE EXPLORATION

· ·

Abigail Saves the Day (1 Samuel 25:2-42)

Say: **Normally a prince of Israel would only take advice from a select few people—and they would only give advice if he asked for it. But that's not what happened in today's Bible passage. This important advice came to David from someone he wouldn't normally listen to at all. Furthermore, this person stopped David when he was in full battle mode and made him listen!**

Ask:

• **Describe what kind of person you think could stop David and give him advice when he didn't want it.**

• **Tell what you think this person might look like.**

Say: **Well, I'm not giving you any more hints, because I've invited someone from David's royal household to tell the story. This person, being royal, is always treated with great respect. Are you ready to respectfully meet a member of David's royal family? Be sure to show every courtesy!**

Go to the door and open it just a crack so kids can't see who's outside. Bow respectfully, then make a sweeping gesture, inviting Lady Abigail into your room. When she approaches the kids, set out a chair for her and cover it with a beautiful cloth. Then back away and take a seat with the children to listen as Abigail speaks.

Prep Box

Ask a woman volunteer to play the role of Abigail. Give your volunteer a copy of "Abigail's Script" (pp. 104-106) early in the week. Have her dress in a Bible-times costume. Because Abigail was wealthy, she might wear colorful scarves and gold or silver bracelets. Encourage your volunteer to carry the script inside a scarf or scroll. Have your Abigail waiting outside the room for you to open the door and introduce her.

Abigail's Script

Enter the room regally, giving a nod toward the
children. Take a seat in the chair the teacher provides.

Shalom! Thank you for inviting me to your class, young servants of the living
God.

I'm Abigail, wife of David, warrior of God, prince of Israel. The day I first met
Prince David I had no idea of marrying him. I was already married, in fact, to
a wealthy but evil man named Nabal. No, when I met David I was thinking of
nothing but saving my family and everyone in my household from David's
anger. He and most of his men were in full battle mode, marching toward my
home, intent on killing everyone in it.

You've probably learned that David was a great man of God who showed
mercy. He was all of those things! But my husband, Nabal, was not. You see,
it was sheepshearing season, a time of celebration and feasts and sharing.
My wealthy husband owned flocks in every direction. While our servants
sheared the sheep, David's men watched over them so that no harm came
to them by day or night. We didn't ask David to do this—he did it out of the
kindness of his heart.

Finally, when the shearing was done and the feasting began, David sent
messengers to my husband, asking if he would share food from the feasting.
David had over 600 men living with him in the wilderness. It would have been
common courtesy for Nabal to pack several donkeys with food and send
them off to David in thanks for watching over our men and our sheep.

But my husband was never courteous. He was proud and spiteful. Rather
than sharing food with David, he sent an insulting response, calling David an
outlaw. David was no outlaw! He'd been anointed by God to be Israel's next
king! To insult God's anointed was like insulting God himself.

My husband's terrible response stirred deep anger within Prince David.
David wouldn't stand for someone to insult him or God. The kind of insult

my husband sent to David demanded a response, and David was ready to deliver one—by sword! He told his men that by nightfall the next day not one male in Nabal's household would be left alive. He and his men strapped on their swords and set out for my home, ready for battle.

I didn't know what had happened until one of our male servants came rushing to me in a panic and told me everything. He was scared to death. Everyone knew that David and his mighty men had never been defeated in battle. And we were no army! We were just a large, wealthy household run by a foolish man.

I knew I had to do something and do it fast. I got all my servants busy in the kitchen. Before long they were loading donkeys with gifts for David and his men—200 loaves of bread, raisins, fig cakes, and sheep meat all ready for roasting—all the good things my kitchen could produce.

I sent the loaded donkeys ahead of me, led by servants. Then I followed on the last donkey, ready to throw myself on David's mercy, to make apologies, and to plead with him to spare our household.

God gave me the courage to set out to meet David and his men that night. If you tried, you could not imagine fiercer-looking warriors. Once there was a time when David and his men set out to fight our enemies, the Philistines. Just the sight of David and his men made our enemies run away—and those were armed, trained Philistines! I was just one woman, facing down the fiercest warrior of our time. My heart was in my throat. With every step my donkey took, I prayed for God to fill me with courage beyond any human courage I'd ever known.

I barely looked at David's face. When I reached the great leader I slipped off my donkey and bowed all the way down to the ground. "My Lord," I said, "please forgive me. I didn't know of your young men who came to my house or of my husband's foolish answer. Please receive these gifts and show mercy to my household, for God will make you and your family great on the throne because you are fighting the Lord's battles. Don't shed blood today and let it be a bad mark on your record!"

I held my breath, waiting for David to answer...

Published in *All Together Now, Volume 4* by Group Publishing, Inc., 1515 Cascade Ave., Loveland, CO 80538.

Finally he said, "Praise the Lord, the God of Israel for sending you out to meet me today! Thank God for your good sense! You've kept me from shedding blood. Now return home in safety. No one will hurt your family."

I was so relieved! I bowed again before the future king, then took my servants and went home. I found my husband in the middle of a great feast. He had no idea how close danger had come. But he had drunk too much, so I didn't tell him until the next morning.

When I told my husband everything that had happened with David, he had a stroke. He could not speak or move, so we put him to bed. He died 10 days later. It was not a sad death—he was mean and stingy and everyone in my house had been afraid of him.

I was surprised to see messengers arrive from David a few days later. You'll never guess what they said—David wanted me to become his wife! I had to catch my breath. *David wanted me to marry him?*

 I quickly gathered my things and five of my maidservants and traveled back with David's servants. In my wildest dreams I never thought of marrying the warrior prince. I had met him only once—when I was begging for the lives of everyone in my household! But this time I was traveling to meet my groom!

Praise God, who is faithful to those who love him! I dared to challenge a prince, knowing he would not want blood on his hands the rest of his life. God took the life of my stingy, sinful husband and placed me in the household of the king! I will forever tell of God's faithfulness and of the kindness of my husband, Prince David!

Exit the room.

Published in *All Together Now, Volume 4* by Group Publishing, Inc., 1515 Cascade Ave., Loveland, CO 80538.

Ask:

• **What did you think about the person God sent to guide David?**

• **Why do you think David listened to Abigail?**

Say: **David was chosen by God and anointed to be the next king of Israel. He didn't *have* to listen to anyone but God. But he *chose* to listen to a woman named Abigail. David realized that ★ *God sends wise people into our lives to guide us.***

Ask:

• **Why was it a good or a bad thing that David chose to listen to Abigail?**

Say: **God's guidance may not always come from a teacher or leader. Sometimes it might come from a friend, or even from a younger brother or sister. God can use people's words to remind us of the truth taught in the Bible.**

Even a great leader like David could humble himself to listen to wisdom from someone else—that means we can, too.

LIFE APPLICATION
. . . .
Thankful Listeners

Say: **Let's talk about people who've given you wise guidance.**

Ask:

• **When have you ever received wise guidance from someone you didn't expect it from?**

Say: **★ *God sends wise people into our lives to guide us,* and we never know just who those people might be. I bet some of those people who regularly guide us might enjoy getting a thank-you. They might even be happily surprised and encouraged!**

Lead kids to your craft area. Lead kids through these simple instructions for cutting and folding the card.

✓ Cut out the card on the solid line. Fold it in half vertically so the print shows.

✓ Fold the pop-up section back and forth on the dotted lines; then open the card and lay it flat.

Prep Box

Prepare a "Bouquet of Thanks Card" as a sample for kids to see and handle. Set out copies of the "Bouquet of Thanks Card" handout (p. 108), scissors, colored pencils, glue sticks, and, if you wish, 4x5-inch envelopes.

Bouquet of Thanks Card

Make this "happy balloon bouquet of thanks" pop-up for someone who has guided you!

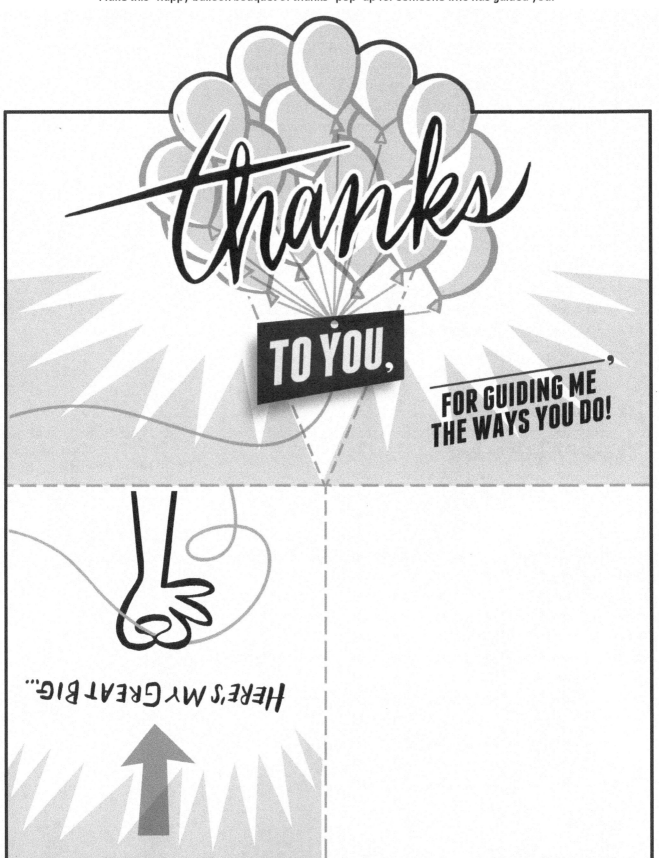

thanks

TO YOU,

FOR GUIDING ME
THE WAYS YOU DO!

HERE'S MY GREAT BIG...

 Published in *All Together Now, Volume 4* by Group Publishing, Inc., 1515 Cascade Ave., Loveland, CO 80538.

✓ Fold the card in half horizontally so the pop-up section faces you. As you fold the card closed, pull the pop-up section toward you.

Note: The card will be folded at the bottom and open at the top.

Have kids use colored pencils to finish the balloons with a bright color scheme. Once the cards are finished, have kids sign their names and then use a glue stick to seal the edges of the card together, being careful to leave the pop-up section free. Hand out envelopes, if you have them, when the glue has dried.

COMMITMENT

Cards to Go

As kids work, brainstorm with them who might receive their cards. Have them write the name on the line inside the card. If kids are making cards for people in your church, encourage them to deliver their cards before they leave church today.As kids finish making their cards, have them clean up the craft area. Then gather everyone in a circle with their finished cards.

Say: ★ ***God sends wise people into our lives to guide us. Sometimes those wise people come from surprising places.***

Ask:

• **How can we remember to listen for the guides God sends our way?**

Say: **Remember, God is always looking for people who are willing to listen to him. Keep your heart open to God. Check in with God just by listening a few times each day.**

Ask:

• **When are times you can check in with God with a silent listening prayer?**

Affirm their ideas and encourage them to pray to God every day.

CLOSING

Prayer for Guidance

Pray: **God, thank you for** ★ *sending wise people into our lives to guide us.* **Help us to be ready to listen like David was willing to listen to Abigail. Keep our hearts open and tender toward you. In Jesus' name, amen.**

David Rules!

LESSON AIM

To help kids know how ★ *King David points the way to Jesus.*

OBJECTIVES

Kids will

✓ play a game of Point the Way,

✓ interactively learn about David's life through 2 Samuel and Psalm 18,

✓ explore how King David points the way to Jesus, and

✓ crown themselves as a reminder that Jesus is their king.

BIBLE BASIS

 2 Samuel 5–7; Psalm 18; Isaiah 9:7

After Saul and his son Jonathan died in a battle with the Philistines, David mourned them and showed them great honor. Then, after inquiring of God, he went to Hebron where the people of Judah proclaimed him king. In the north, however, with the support of Saul's army, Saul's remaining son Ishbosheth ruled for a time until his own people eventually killed him. Finally, after years of exercising amazing patience, David ascended the throne of Israel at the age of 37. He defeated Israel's enemies on all sides and expanded her borders. For the first time, God's people lived in peace and safety.

David demonstrated extraordinary self-restraint in his unwillingness to shed the blood of any of Saul's family to gain access

You'll need...

- ☐ bag of small treats such as doughnut holes or sugarless gum*
- ☐ blindfolds
- ☐ baking sheet
- ☐ wooden spoon
- ☐ brightly colored construction paper
- ☐ washable black markers
- ☐ copy of the "Psalm 18, David's Song" handout (p. 116)
- ☐ easy-to-read version of the Bible
- ☐ copies of the "King David to King Jesus" handout (p.120) on heavy yellow paper
- ☐ scissors
- ☐ cellophane tape
- ☐ optional: glitter glue, hairdryer

* Always check for allergies before serving snacks.

to the throne God had promised him when he was just a young shepherd. This is one of our first indications that David would be no ordinary king, but a king for the ages—a king whose reign gives us a foreshadowing of what the Messiah's reign will be like. He was a king after God's own heart, whom God established as a direct ancestor of Jesus.

Jesus would quote David's words from the Psalms more than any other Old Testament source. In some cases, such as Psalm 22, it seems that David could have been praying the very thoughts of Jesus 1,000 years in our linear sense of time before Jesus prayed them on the cross. What was this baffling yet undeniable connection between our Jesus and the remarkable king of Israel? We can observe and explore it, but we can't presume to explain it. However, when all is said and done, we can see that David clearly points the way to Jesus.

Of course David, as a fallen man, sinned, repented wholeheartedly, and yet paid dearly in consequences for his foolish actions, while Jesus lived a perfect life in order to become the perfect sacrifice for our sins. With that all-important fact held in the balance, look at these astonishing similarities between Jesus and David.

✓ Both were born in Bethlehem.

✓ Both came out of nowhere and rose to power.

✓ Both astounded people when they were young: David and Goliath, Jesus at the Temple when he was 12.

✓ David was a shepherd; Jesus is regarded as the Good Shepherd.

✓ David's success made Saul fear him and plot against him; Jesus' miracles and popularity with the people made the religious establishment fear him and plot against him.

✓ David saved his people from their enemies; Jesus saved his people from their sins.

✓ Saul set traps for David; the Pharisees set traps for Jesus.

That's just a sampling of the comparisons that can be made, but that list in itself is astounding.

God chose David to be the future king, even with David's weaknesses. God knew there would be times David would fall short, but also knew that David would turn back to him in solemn repentance and mend his ways. David's *mind* and *heart* were always attuned to God—we can see that in the heart cries he recorded in his psalms,

All Together Now

which remain breathtakingly contemporary. It's unusual for a warrior of David's ferocity to display such tenderness of heart toward God, such skill in music and literature, such overall charisma. All these gifts David used not for his own glory, but for God's—setting the stage for a far greater King to follow.

📖 Mark 11:9-10

This passage in Mark is part of the familiar account of Palm Sunday, Jesus' triumphal entry into Jerusalem. After remaining mostly anonymous during his three-year ministry, Jesus goes up to Jerusalem for one last Passover, knowing that before the week is out he will give his life for the sins of the world.

The joyous crowd gives Jesus a king's welcome with the laying of robes and palm branches, all the while quoting...a psalm, of course! They clearly recognize Jesus as the promised Messiah and call out, "Blessings on the coming Kingdom of our ancestor David!"

Christians sometimes study the Bible from the time of Jesus backward. If we take the richer path of beginning at the beginning, we see the deep lines King David traced in history, lines that pointed toward Jesus who would become the savior of the world.

UNDERSTANDING YOUR KIDS

Heroes come and heroes go. Kids today are taught to question and challenge why Jesus is different from any other great teacher in history. This lesson provides great assurance toward that point.

Jesus didn't just casually drop into history at some random time and place. God foreshadowed his coming by leaving clues in the history of his people Israel. God gave them a great king named David who was obedient to the greater king of heaven. God gave David remarkable insights into the far greater King who would come after him—a savior not of the state of Israel, but a savior for the world who would be worshipped by all nations (Psalm 86:9).

This savior Jesus, son of David, Son of God, is *the* one we can trust with our hearts and lives. He is God's plan for us. By faith in him we are adopted into the royal family as well.

THE LESSON »

ATTENTION GRABBER

Point the Way

Give kids a warm greeting. Explain that you have treats hiding somewhere, but that kids will have to work to find them! Ask kids to choose a Leader. Have the rest of the kids line up behind the Leader. Distribute blindfolds and have kids help each other put them on securely, including the Leader.

Say: **Here's how you'll find the treats. Put your hands on the waist of the person in front of you. Leader, put your hands on your own waist. I'm going to step away in the direction of the treat. I won't talk anymore, but I will make a noise for you to follow.**

Leader, do your best to point the group toward the noise. Every few seconds I'll make the noise again. Keep following the noise. Eventually the noise will lead you to the treats.

Since you can't see the ground beneath you, take small, careful steps. You never know where I might lead you.

Back away several feet from the kids, and then bang the baking sheet with the wooden spoon three times. Pause a moment; then bang the baking sheet again.

Wait for the kids to follow you. Staying a good distance from them, bang the baking sheet every few seconds. Be sure to bang it three times, pause, and then bang it three more times. The second set of three bangs helps the blindfolded kids be a little more sure of their bearings.

Make your adventure as complex as you like, keeping in mind that you'll not want to expose the kids to changes in footing such as stairs while they're blindfolded. When you arrive at the treats, give the final pairs of bangs while the kids are still several feet away. Let them stop in confusion before you bang your signal again.

When kids arrive at your location and the treats, say: **You're here! Take off your blindfolds and enjoy!**

Pass out the treats for everyone to enjoy on the way back to your room. When you're back, form a discussion circle and ask:

• **Describe what it was like to follow my sound signals.**

• **What about when I stopped giving signals?**

• **Leader, tell how you felt about leading everyone when you couldn't see where you were going.**

Say: **Today we're going to learn what happened when David became king of Israel. He'd waited a long time since Samuel had anointed him when he was a young shepherd.**

Prep Box

Hide a bag of treats some distance from your teaching space. You may want to take this adventure outside or into a neighboring room.

Teacher Tip

Have an adult volunteer walk as a guide beside the blindfolded kids to help them over any obstacles in their path.

All Together Now

But David was patient and followed God, even when the way was confusing and God seemed far away. Not only will we see how David became Israel's greatest leader, we'll see the many ways ★ *King David points the way to Jesus.*

BIBLE EXPLORATION

David Rules! (2 Samuel 5–7; Psalm 18; Isaiah 9:7)

Say: **Every now and then the Bible gives us a special person to learn about—someone so important, so faithful to God that he or she changed the course of history. I'm going to let you in on a little secret. King David was one of those people! Because David's heart was so close to God, God blessed him. In the end, ★ *David points the way to Jesus.* And God promised David that his reign would last forever, because God's own Son would be born from David's family 1,000 years after David ruled.**

Ask:

• **Describe what you know about David's life so far.**

Encourage kids to lay out as much of David's life as they can, including being chosen by God to be Israel's next king, believing that God was stronger than Goliath, refusing to harm his enemy Saul when he had the chance, and listening to a wise woman God put in his path to keep him from shedding blood.

Say: **Let's hear from David himself how he felt about God rescuing him from King Saul.**

Have a willing child read aloud Psalm 18, Part 1.

Say: **We know David was quite a unique person. But a lot of the most important adventures with David happened before he even became king. Today we're going to look at what happened when David ruled. And we're going to borrow part of the story from words David wrote himself.**

Besides being a great harp player, singer, leader, warrior, and follower of God, David also wrote beautiful songs. And we still sing a lot of David's songs today. Those songs are called *psalms,* **and they're in the Bible in the book of Psalms. When you read those psalms, little phrases will jump out and you'll think,** *Hey—I've heard that before!* **And you'll be right.**

In fact, the Bible calls David "the sweet psalmist of Israel" (2 Samuel 23:1). **This was** *some king!*

Prep Box

Cut apart the four parts of the "Psalm 18, David's Song" handout (p. 116), and tuck them in this guide. Set out half-sheets of colorful construction paper and washable black markers. Mark 2 Samuel 5 in an easy-to-read version of the Bible.

Teacher Tip

Be prepared to name favorite praise songs you sing in your church that contain phrases from psalms.

Psalm 18, David's Song

Psalm 18, Part 1

3 I called on the Lord, who is worthy of praise, and he saved me from my enemies.

5 The grave wrapped its ropes around me; death laid a trap in my path.

6 But in my distress I cried out to the Lord...He heard me from his sanctuary; my cry to him reached his ears.

17 He rescued me from my powerful enemies, from those who hated me and were too strong for me.

Psalm 18, Part 2

19 He led me to a place of safety; he rescued me because he delights in me.

20 The Lord rewarded me for doing right; he restored me because of my innocence.

21 For I have kept the ways of the Lord; I have not turned from my God to follow evil.

22 I have followed all his regulations; I have never abandoned his decrees.

Psalm 18, Part 3

28 The Lord, my God, lights up my darkness.

29 In your strength I can crush an army; with my God I can scale any wall.

32 God arms me with strength, and he makes my way perfect.

34 He trains my hands for battle; he strengthens my arm to draw a bronze bow.

35 You have given me your shield of victory. Your right hand supports me; your help has made me great.

Psalm 18, Part 4

43 You appointed me ruler over nations; people I don't even know now serve me.

46 The Lord lives! Praise to my Rock! May the God of my salvation be exalted!

49 For this, O Lord, I will praise you among the nations; I will sing praises to your name.

50 You give great victories to your king; you show unfailing love to your anointed, to David and all his descendants forever.

Published in *All Together Now, Volume 4* by Group Publishing, Inc., 1515 Cascade Ave., Loveland, CO 80538.

We know that as long as King Saul was alive, David would never take Israel's throne from him. One day Saul and his son Jonathan were killed in a battle with the Philistines. Some people thought David would be happy that Saul was finally dead. But they were wrong. David made sure that Saul and Jonathan received an honorable burial. He and all his soldiers mourned for them. David even wrote a psalm about them and sang it.

This psalm is in 2 Samuel 1:19-27. I'll read you a part of it.

Your pride and joy, O Israel, lies dead on the hills! Oh, how the mighty heroes have fallen!...The bow of Jonathan was power-ful, and the sword of Saul did its mighty work...How beloved and gracious were Saul and Jonathan! They were together in life and in death. They were swifter than eagles, stronger than lions. O women of Israel, weep for Saul...Oh, how the mighty heroes have fallen in battle! Jonathan lies dead on the hills. How I weep for you, my brother Jonathan!...Oh, how the mighty heroes have fallen!

Ask:

• **Describe what surprises you about what David wrote in this psalm about the man who'd tried to kill him.**

Say: **This is one of the outstanding things about David. He was merciful. Even though he had spent several years of his life running from Saul, David had only kind things to say when Saul died.**

Ask:

• **How do you think David could be so kind to the one who'd tried to kill him?**

Say: **The Bible tells us that when David was anointed, God sent his Spirit on David and God's Spirit remained with him.**

Ask:

• **How do you think God's Spirit would make a difference in how David acted?**

Say: **Let's write some words that describe David on these bright sheets of paper.** Let kids come up and write or draw things they think describe David, one word or phrase per half-sheet of paper.

Say: **After Saul died, God told David to go live in the town of Hebron. After years and years of living in the wilderness, David and his men found all kinds of comforts in a town. Let's find out what David himself had to say about this in Psalm 18.**

Have a willing child read aloud Psalm 18, Part 2.

Say: **The people of Judah anointed David as their king. But Saul's army was not ready to give up its power after Saul died. In the northern part of the country, Saul's general put Saul's son Ishbosheth on the throne. Everyone try saying Ishbosheth with me. It's kind of like sneezing! Here we go: Ishbosheth!**

Ishbosheth wasn't really much of a king. It was really general Abner who was in charge. The land of Israel remained divided for seven years, with Ishbosheth king in the north and David king in the south.

One day general Abner got angry at Ishbosheth and decided to go over to David's side. Then two of Ishbosheth's own leaders killed him. David mourned the death of Ishbosheth just as he had mourned the death of Saul.

Before long, the leaders of northern Israel came to David. Let's see what the northern leaders had to say to David.

Have a willing child read 2 Samuel 5:1-5.

David was king in Judah for a long time before he eventually became king of all Israel. He had to wait many years to rule, even though he had been chosen by God as a child.

Ask:

• What other words describing David could we add to our list?

Say: **So finally, when David was 37 years old, he became king over all Israel. Then great things began to happen. He conquered Israel's enemies on all sides. He conquered the people who held the city of Jerusalem and made it his capital city. He talks about his battles in Psalm 18.**

Have a willing child read Psalm 18, Part 3.

Say: **Kings of other countries sent David gifts to help him build his palace and the city of Jerusalem, which became known as "the city of David." Israel enjoyed peace for the first time. Under David's rule, many people turned to God. Let's hear how David rejoices.**

Have a willing child read Psalm 18, Part 4.

Ask:

• What other words could we add to our colorful collection of words about David?

Say: **We've learned a lot about David today. But more important, let's look at how ★ *King David points the way to Jesus.* And let's look at how we, too, can be people "after God's own heart."**

LIFE APPLICATION
. . . .
From King to King of Kings

Have kids arrange the words about David in a large circle and then stand inside the circle. Invite the kids to take turns reading the words aloud. Then ask:

• **How do these words remind you of another important person in the Bible?**

Let kids mention all the Bible persons who come to mind. Ask:

• **Can you think of ways David and Jesus were alike and ways they were different?**

Say: **Even though David was just a man and Jesus is God's Son, ★ *King David points the way to Jesus.* One way they were the same is that David was a shepherd and Jesus called himself the Good Shepherd. David showed us in all these ways** (gesture to the words) **what Jesus would be like. David saved the nation of Israel from its enemies. Jesus saved the world from its sin.**

One way Jesus and David were different is that David lived as king for 40 years while Jesus reigns forever. David was a king; Jesus is the King of kings. David had a heart for God, so he gave us a little glimpse of what Jesus would be like.

The most important way David and Jesus were different is that David was human, so sometimes he sinned and asked God's forgiveness. But Jesus lived a perfect life so he could be the sacrifice for our sins.

Help kids complete their crowns according to the instructions on the handout. If you choose to use glitter glue, allow kids to put very light lines of it around the jewels after the crown is assembled. Have an adult helper or an older child supervise the use of a hair dryer to dry the glitter glue.

Prep Box

Set out scissors, markers, and copies of the "King David to King Jesus" handout (p. 120). You may also use these optional supplies: glitter glue and a hair dryer.

COMMITMENT
. . . .
Who's Your King?

Before kids put on their crowns, say: **King David was a great ruler in Israel. He loved God with all his heart. Rather than grabbing for power, he patiently followed God's instructions.**

King David to King Jesus

Decorate the front of the crown. Cut the three pieces of the crown apart on the heavy lines. Tape the two pieces of the back of the crown together and tape one side of the back of the crown to the front. Your teacher will tape the other side of the back of the crown in place so it fits just right. Carefully cut off any extra length from the back of the crown.

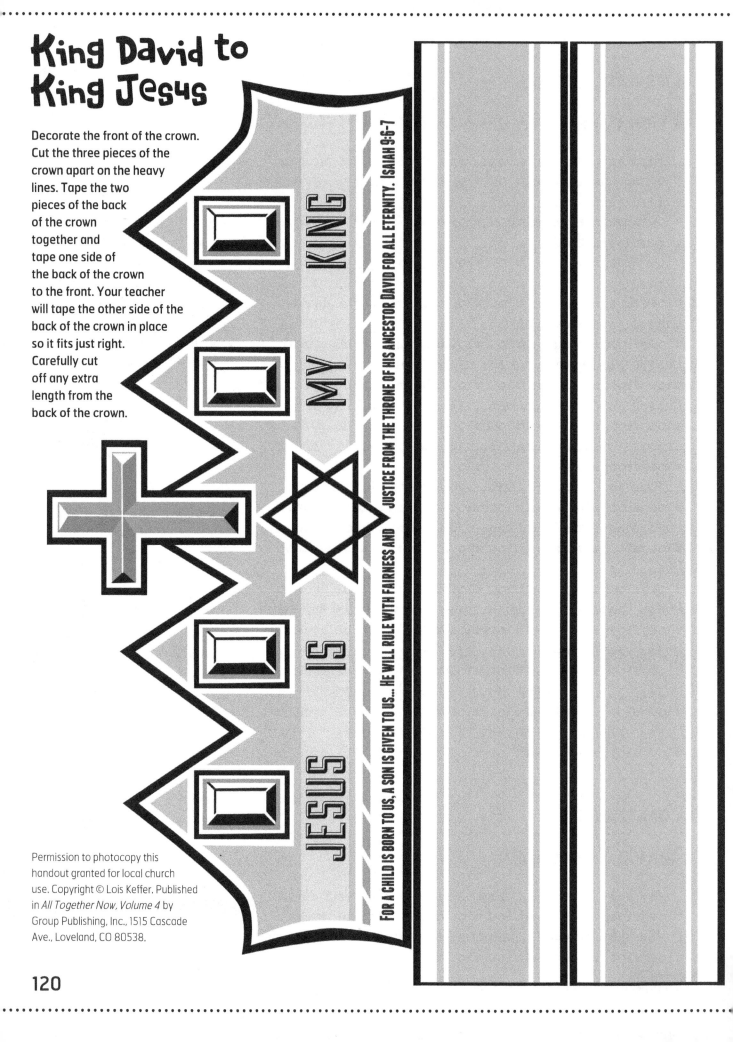

KING

MY

IS

JESUS

FOR A CHILD IS BORN TO US, A SON IS GIVEN TO US... HE WILL RULE WITH FAIRNESS AND JUSTICE FROM THE THRONE OF HIS ANCESTOR DAVID FOR ALL ETERNITY. ISAIAH 9:6-7

He showed mercy and kindness to his enemies. He brought peace to his nation. In these ways, ★ *King David points the way to Jesus.* He gave us a little glimpse of what the King of kings would be like.

Ask:

• **What does it mean to have Jesus be king of your life?**

This is an excellent place to invite children to place their lives in Jesus' hands according to your church's tradition. Then, as a step of faith, have them crown themselves with Jesus as king of their lives. For those who have already put their trust in Jesus, crowning themselves can be a celebration of their faith.

CLOSING

Sing It!

Say: **Congratulations on all you've discovered today as you've learned how** ★ *King David points the way to Jesus.* **I think this calls for a celebration!**

Lead kids in singing a praise song they all know.

Showdown on Mount Carmel

LESSON AIM

To help kids know that ★ *nothing is impossible with God.*

OBJECTIVES

Kids will

✓ play a game of The Lone Guard,

✓ do a live newscast of the dramatic events on Mount Carmel,

✓ create a paper spiral to represent Elijah's flames, and

✓ be challenged to believe that nothing is impossible with God.

BIBLE BASIS

 1 Kings 18

Israel has a *baaaaad* king. The worst. According to 1 Kings 16:30-31:

But Ahab son of Omri did what was evil in the Lord's sight, even more than any of the kings before him. And as though it were not enough to follow the example of Jeroboam, he married Jezebel, the daughter of King Ethbaal of the Sidonians, and he began to bow down in worship of Baal.

When the Bible names someone the baddest of the bad, you know it's not a pretty situation.

You'll need...

- ☐ clean, empty 1-liter bottle
- ☐ used office paper
- ☐ 2 aluminum pie pans
- ☐ large sheets of newsprint
- ☐ markers
- ☐ toy microphone or paper towel tube
- ☐ copy of the "News Clips" handout (p. 131)
- ☐ copies of the Bible in an easy-to-read version
- ☐ copies of the "Elijah's Flames" handout (p. 132)
- ☐ scissors
- ☐ markers or colored pencils
- ☐ pencils
- ☐ transparent tape
- ☐ optional: smart phone or video device for recording

To face Ahab, God brings forth an extraordinary prophet: Elijah. When I get to heaven, I look forward to meeting Elijah. He's full of God's power and the kind of in-your-face attitude required to get the attention of a scoundrel like Ahab.

Queen Jezebel certainly egged on Ahab in all his anti-Yahweh activities. Indeed, she may have exceeded him. Ahab built a temple for Baal in his capital at Samaria and also set up an Asherah pole. Worship of these idols included temple prostitutes. The Baals were supposedly gods of fertility and rain. In their debauchery, people thought they were assuring fertility for their animals and crops. This behavior was a supremely seductive and entertaining rite for the people of Israel, especially when promoted by the king and his queen in place of pure-hearted worship of God. It was this very sort of worship that God urged Joshua and the Israelites to stomp out when they first conquered the Promised Land.

Queen Jezebel took Ahab's promotion of the false gods of Canaan a step further. This treacherous daughter of the Phoenician king actually set out to kill all of God's prophets (1 Kings 18:4). In essence, through her actions, she took on the God of the universe. Did she really think of herself as invincible? Had the daughter of a powerful king been so used to getting her way that she thought nothing was beyond her control? Her very name has come to symbolize evil, and rightly so.

God inserted a single prophetic voice to confront these two wicked characters who assumed leadership of Israel. The lone prophet Elijah declared that because of Ahab's wickedness, not a drop of rain would fall in Israel for several years. As the drought deepened, Jezebel had people searching everywhere to destroy the "troublemaker of Israel." But Elijah returned in God's own time, on God's own terms.

And his purpose? To issue a challenge. Let all the prophets of Baal pray for fire to fall on their sacrifice. Then he alone would pray for God to send fire to consume his own water-soaked sacrifice.

Elijah upped the ante against himself because he knew that nothing is impossible for God. The prophets of Baal worked themselves into a frenzy, but heard nothing from their nothing god. Elijah's prayer called down fire from God that consumed not only the sacrifice, but all the water poured on it and the stones of the altar itself. The people seized the false prophets and gave them to Elijah, who killed them. And before the day was out, God sent rain.

Interestingly, all this takes place on the mountain overlooking the valley of Megiddo, the prophesied scene of the final battle of good and evil. There's no doubt about who wins that battle either.

All Together Now

📖 Mark 10:23-27

The concept that nothing is impossible with God appears a few times in the New Testament. In this case, the rich young ruler had just walked away from Jesus sadly, unable to give away his riches and follow Jesus. Jesus made the statement to his disciples, "It is easier for a camel to go through the eye of a needle than for a rich person to enter the Kingdom of God."

The overwhelmed disciples then asked in despair, "Then who in the world can be saved?"

Jesus answered, "What is impossible for people is possible with God."

Elijah certainly had every confidence in this truth. With 850 prophets of Baal and Asherah against his solo priestly performance before God, with parameters of an all-or-nothing provision of fire from heaven, with a king looking on who was just itching to kill him—Elijah placed himself utterly in the category of those who bet their lives on the fact that God could indeed do what was impossible for humans.

What a prophet! What a God! What a showdown for the ages.

UNDERSTANDING YOUR KIDS

Believing in a God who can do anything automatically brings the why questions.

If God can do anything, then why did he let Mom die?

If God can do anything, then why didn't he stop that terrible storm that killed so many people?

If God can do anything, then why doesn't he give me more friends?

These are questions we can encourage from our kids—God is certainly up to these challenges and more. Kids who work through difficult questions such as these develop a much stronger faith than those who are forced to stuff their questions and simply buy the church's "line."

Jesus tells us that the rain falls on the just and the unjust alike (Matthew 5:45). Being followers of Jesus gives us no pass to a pain-free life—we face the same challenges and heart-rending experiences that people without faith do. We can teach kids that God uses these times to draw us closer to him. We can tell them how Jesus cried when his dear friend Lazarus, Mary and Martha's brother, died. We can explain that if God were to give Christians a free pass from painful experiences, people would become Christians not out of love for God, but for personal gain.

Second, we teach kids that although God *can* do anything, we live in a fallen world. God may let the consequences of sin run their natural course. God let his own Son, Jesus, die to save the people of the world from their sins.

In the case of Elijah on Mount Carmel, God interfered with the laws of nature to turn the hearts of a lost nation back to him.

Use this lesson to teach kids that while nothing is impossible with God, we trust him in his sovereignty whether he intervenes on our behalf or not.

All Together Now

ATTENTION GRABBER

The Lone Guard

Greet kids by name and ask if they're ready for a super-fun game.

Have everyone form a large circle. Stand an empty one-liter bottle in the center of the circle. Distribute sheets of used office paper. Tell kids to make paper balls of their sheets of paper.

Then say: **I need a brave volunteer to be the lone guard of our helpless bottle here in the center of the circle.** Hold up the two aluminum pie pans. **You'll be able to use these two pie pans as well as your body to guard the bottle as everyone else throws their paper balls at it. Who's up for the task?**

Choose a willing child. Explain that the guard may not touch the bottle with the pie pans—just use them to hover around it, kind of like shields.

Let the kids in the circle throw their paper balls when you say "Go." Have the guard continue until the bottle has been knocked over twice. Then let the guard choose another guard. Continue until everyone has had a chance to play guard. Then have everyone sit down.

Ask:

• **Describe how you felt when you failed to protect the bottle and it fell down.**

• **Tell about how it felt to have everyone else playing against you.**

• **Suppose there were 850 people playing against you. What do you think it would be like to be the guard?**

Say: **That would be pretty overwhelming. But that's what it was like for the hero in our Bible passage today. He was the only one on God's side against an evil king and queen and more than 800 priests who believed in false gods. And what's more, our hero is the one who challenged them! He was absolutely fearless because he knew that ★ *nothing is impossible with God.***

BIBLE EXPLORATION

Showdown! (1 Kings 18)

Explain to kids that today's Bible passage was quite a story in its time. In fact, it was probably the biggest news story in 10 or 20 years. Tell kids you'll give them the basic setup, and then it will be their job to tell the rest of the story from the News Clips you give them straight from the Bible. Here's the setup.

Say: **King Ahab ruled on the throne of Israel. He was the *worst* king Israel had ever known.** Have kids "boo" for Ahab. **Ahab didn't worship the God of Israel. He was an idol worshipper who led people away from God and set up idol worship right in front of his palace.** Have kids give more "boos."

His wife Queen Jezebel was even worse! She was the daughter of a foreign king. She was dead set against the God of Israel. She even tried to have all the prophets of God killed. Have kids "boo" Jezebel. **Whatever bad things King Ahab did, Jezebel encouraged him to do even worse things.**

The poor country of Israel was in terrible shape. It was nothing like it had been under the great King David. God chose one man—just one man—who was strong and brave enough to stand up to this evil king and queen. His name was Elijah. Elijah was a great prophet.

One day Elijah stood up to King Ahab and said, "Because of all the evil you've done, there will be no rain in the land of Israel for the next few years until I give the word." Then Elijah disappeared to a place where God cared for him.

Ask:

• **Tell about a time when the weather was hot and we needed rain.**

Say: **There was no rain for *three years!* King Ahab was furious with Elijah. Elijah had been hiding, but he knew the time was right to come meet Ahab face to face.**

That's as far as I'm going to tell you. Now it's your turn. You'll form three News Crews. I'll give each crew one part of the story from the Bible. You can decide together how to tell it. Will you do a live newscast from the site? Will you interview someone who was there? Will you draw newsprint pictures to show how the story unfolded? Will you use two news anchors and a live reporter?

We'll use this (indicate your paper towel tube or microphone) **as a microphone. You can choose a desk and chair to be your news desk.**

Prep Box

Cut apart the three pieces of the "News Clips" handout (p. 131) and tuck them in this guide. Have Bibles in an easy-to-read version, large newsprint, markers, and a toy microphone or paper towel tube available to the kids. If you wish, record kids' news reports on your smartphone or other video device.

All Together Now

Get together with your News Crew, study the Scripture, and then decide how you'll present it as a news story to the rest of the group. I'll give you a few minutes to prepare. Let's see how you report on the facts of this memorable day in Israel's history.

Help kids form three News Crews, making sure each crew has a good blend of kids. Then send the crews to different parts of the room to create their news stories. You and another adult volunteer can visit the News Crews to make sure they understand their Bible passages and are generating good ideas about how to present the stories to the rest of the group.

When crews have had ample time to prepare, give them a two-minute warning so they can gather their things and prepare to "go live." Then have the crews make their presentations in order. Give each crew a hearty round of applause before proceeding to the next crew.

Say: **Great reporting! Now I have one further challenge for you. It's time to turn your News Crews into investigative reporting teams. Get back into your crews and come up with two questions about today's Bible story. Make sure they're deep-thinking questions, not simple questions that people can answer in one word.**

Give the crews about two minutes to come up with their questions, and then bring everyone back together again. Have each News Crew pose questions to the rest of the kids in the group. If kids struggle with questions, ask some yourself.

Say: **It seems as though Elijah had a remarkable amount of courage to take on a challenge like this. That might be the case, but look at it this way, too. Elijah had remarkable faith in God. In fact, Elijah believed that ★ *nothing is impossible with God.***

Ask:

• **Tell what you think the "impossible" thing Elijah had faith that God would do was.**

• **Elijah was outnumbered 850 to one. How do you think he had the courage to challenge all those people?**

• **Why do you think Elijah poured all that water on his sacrifice?**

• **What do you think—can God really do anything?**

Say: **Elijah was one of God's most powerful prophets, called by God to help Israel in dark, dark times. There's no doubt that God sends special people to help his people in special times.**

It's important for you to know that it wasn't the people themselves who were great. It was their faith in God that was great. Elijah's faith was so great that he didn't mind challenging an evil king and 850 false prophets and standing against them *alone*. But he wasn't exactly alone.

Ask:

• Tell who else you think was on Elijah's side—and why.

• How did the people of Israel realize God was on Elijah's side?

Say: **Eventually, Elijah confronted King Ahab again. And again God gave Elijah something difficult to say to the evil king. And again Elijah obeyed, because he knew that ★ *nothing is impossible with God.***

LIFE APPLICATION

Elijah's Flames

Say: **When Elijah asked God to send down flames to burn up the sacrifice that had all that water poured over it, that was a *huge* prayer.**

Ask:

• **Have you ever asked God to answer a huge prayer? How did that work out?**

• **How did God answer Elijah's huge prayer?**

Say: **Today we're going to make a cool craft to remind us of the way God answered Elijah's huge prayer, and also to remind us that ★ *nothing is impossible with God!* But watch out while you work on this craft—it might get a little hot!**

Lead kids to your craft area and show them your completed Elijah's Flames project. Handle it as if it's extremely hot.

Follow the instructions on the handout to complete the spiral of flames. If you have time, let the kids color the flames with colored pencils or markers before they curl them around a pencil. Kids will need help taping the inside tight curl and the outside final curl.

As kids finish their flame spirals, have them help others who are not so quick to finish. Then have everyone help clean up the craft area.

Prep Box

Prepare an example of the Elijah's Flames craft for kids to examine. In your craft area set out scissors, markers or colored pencils, pencils, transparent tape, and copies of the "Elijah's Flames" handout (p. 132). Also, be prepared to tell about a time when God answered a huge prayer for you.

All Together Now

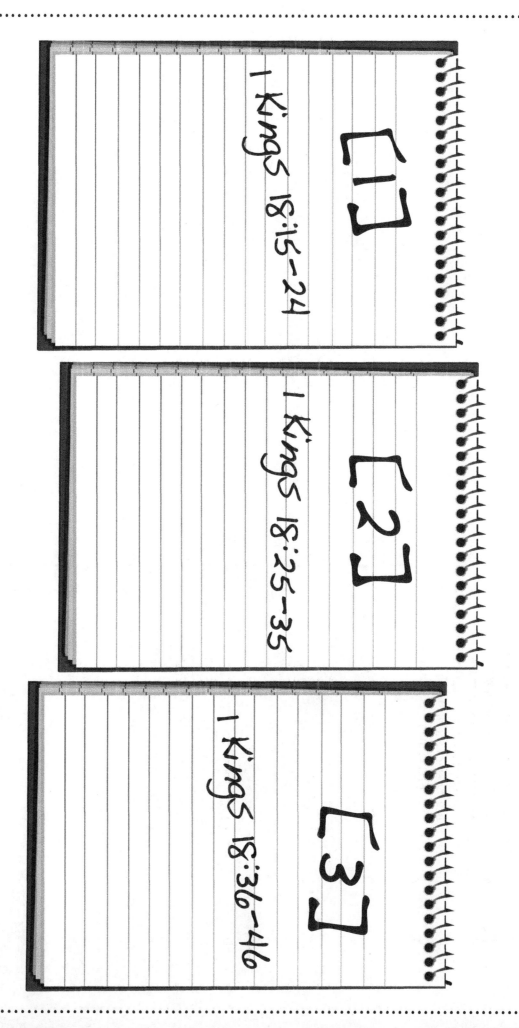

News Clips

[1]

1 Kings 18:15-24

[2]

1 Kings 18:25-35

[3]

1 Kings 18:36-46

Elijah's Flames

Cut out both sets of flames. Overlap them and tape them together on both sides with invisible tape. Roll the flames tightly around a pencil, beginning with the wide end. Remove the pencil, wrap the inner curl tightly and secure it with tape. Let the flames grow in an outward spiral. Bend back the small end on the dotted line. Secure it to an inside layer of the spiral with tape.

* NOTHING IS IMPOSSIBLE WITH GOD * NOTHING IS IMPOSSIBLE WITH GOD * NOTHING IS IMPOSSIBLE WITH GOD * NOTHING IS IMPOSSIBLE WITH GOD *

COMMITMENT
....

All Kinds of Answers

Invite kids to bring their flame spirals and join you in a discussion circle on the floor.

Ask:

• **What do your flame spirals remind you of?**

• **What does it mean if we pray and ask God for something but we don't get what we want?**

Say: **Even though ★ *nothing is impossible with God,* sometimes God has a better idea than we've thought of. It can be difficult when we put a great big prayer out there and God doesn't answer the way we expect.**

We look at how we hope things will be today, tomorrow, and next month. But God looks *way* down the road, 10 and 20 years from now. That's longer than you've even been here. So when God says no to our prayers, he's really saying, "Wait. I have something better."

When that happens, God asks us to hang on to our faith, even though it's difficult. Because we know ★ *nothing is impossible with God.*

If you're willing to hang on to your faith even when God says no to a huge prayer, will you put your flame spiral on your hand and hold it up to glow in the middle of our circle?

Prep Box

Be prepared to share an experience when God *didn't* answer a big prayer the way you hoped, but later—even years later—things turned out for the best.

CLOSING
....

Huge Prayers

Say: **Let's close in prayer. Keep your flames glowing!**

Pray: **Dear Lord, we know that ★ *nothing is impossible with you.* Teach us to pray huge prayers like Elijah did, God. And keep us trusting in you, no matter how you answer. In Jesus' name, amen.**

Elijah Runs Away

You'll need...

- ☐ toaster oven
- ☐ package of refrigerated biscuits or crescent rolls*
- ☐ paper towels
- ☐ copy of the "Elijah's Story Quotes" handout (p. 143)
- ☐ broom
- ☐ copies of the "Packet of Comfort" handout (p. 144)
- ☐ scissors
- ☐ glue sticks
- ☐ raffia

* Always check for allergies before serving snacks.

LESSON AIM

To help kids know that ★ *God comforts us when we're discouraged.*

OBJECTIVES

Kids will

- ✓ tell about times they feel like running away,
- ✓ experience Elijah's retreat from Jezebel's anger, and then discover God's comfort,
- ✓ create a packet of comforting verses from the Bible, and
- ✓ commit to listening for God's still, small voice.

BIBLE BASIS

 **1 Kings 19**

There's one hard-and-sure truth that everyone who serves God runs into sooner or later: We have an enemy who's wily, knows our weaknesses, and is determined to bring us down. Counterbalancing that truth is an even greater one: God understands our weaknesses and comforts us in our troubles.

Elijah provides a stunning example of these truths at play. In one moment, he was defeating hundreds of prophets of Baal and Asherah in a confrontation where their false gods failed to provide fire for their sacrifice—but the God of Israel sent fire that consumed sacrifice, water, and altar. The next moment, this powerful man of God was running until his strength gave out, scared witless of the nasty revenge the godless Queen Jezebel would exact should she get her evil hands on him.

And what happened to the mighty man of God? After winning the showdown, he turned into a coward and didn't stop until he dropped?

Well, yes, that's exactly what happened.

Honesty about its heroes is one of the hallmarks that sets the Bible apart from all other books. If you notice, no "perfect" people are allowed in God's book. The writers of Scripture give them to us warts and all so we can better understand the realities of the high calling that God places on our lives.

Crumpling after a victorious moment for God's kingdom is an occurrence most of us know well. It's as if we use up our entire tank of spiritual energy. Then, before God refills us, while we're at our most vulnerable—BAM!—a spiritual grenade knocks us off our feet.

Nearly every time I feel that I've done something "important" for the kingdom of God, before I can take the next step some character-testing circumstance develops that makes me want to run for the hills.

We have an enemy whose job is to keep us off balance spiritually. He doesn't let those mountaintop experiences last for long. He's clever and knows our points of weakness only too well.

It's possible Elijah's exhaustion and despair were the result of Satan's work. Gone was the exhilarating sense of God's unstoppable power; in its place came dread of a hate-driven queen. It might not make sense. But in Elijah's mind it was real.

But God made, and therefore understood, Elijah. He didn't let Elijah run down that path of fear alone. Not for a minute. And when Elijah was finally ready to listen, God was there to restore the prophet, heal him from his fear, and send him forth with a helper.

If God gets exasperated with our human weaknesses, he doesn't let it show. Rather, he gently leads us along, step by step, until we find ourselves safely in the circle of his arms again.

📖 Luke 12:22-32

After his teachings on the flowers of the field and seeking first the kingdom of God, Jesus adds these words of comfort for his listeners: "Don't be afraid, little flock." These are great words for contemplation. Consider writing them on a sticky note and posting it on a mirror or in another spot where you'll see them several times a day. Or better yet, tuck the words into your heart so you can pull them out and take comfort from them whenever you need comfort.

God had done *huge* work through Elijah, just as God does work through us. Elijah crashed and ran, much as we often do. When those moments happen, remember these gentle words from our Savior: "Don't be afraid, little flock." Remember that Jesus knew all the feelings we know. Lean into his strength and compassion.

UNDERSTANDING YOUR KIDS

Let your mind roll back to your little kid self. Did you ever think about running away? Ever start down the block with your chin jutting out and your "mad" on?

My pastor once told of feeling put out by his parents' discipline, stuffing peanut butter and crackers into a bag, and taking off for greener pastures. He made it about three blocks before he began to question his decision. There sat his father on a park bench, waiting to intercept him, offer his hand, and walk him home. What a tender-hearted picture of the way God deals with us!

Rare is the child who doesn't think of taking off from home for one reason or another. Fortunately, most realize what a scary decision they're making before they get to the door.

Children also run from overwhelming circumstances, much as Elijah did. Better to feign illness when the report isn't done or when a difficult test looms. Sometimes life just seems too much to bear—and the best response kids can think of is to find a way out. (As grown-ups we haven't changed all that much, have we?)

This lesson puts a great truth in your kids' pockets: Before we take our first running-away steps, God is already on a path to intercept us, draw us back into his loving arms, and assure us that we're not alone.

THE LESSON »

To Run or Not

Give kids a warm personal greeting as they arrive. Gather them in a discussion circle and say: **I'm glad you all came here rather than running away from me this morning!**

Ask:

• **Tell whether you've ever thought about running away and why.**

• **When have you actually run from something, like a mean dog?**

• **When might there be a better solution to a problem than running away?**

Say: **Here's something to think about: Even adults sometimes think about running away from things that seem too hard to handle. It's true. Even adults can get so scared about a problem that they think about giving up and running away.**

Even great Bible heroes sometimes felt like running away. That seems a little hard to believe, doesn't it? But it's true. Even some really, truly, amazingly great Bible heroes.

It's a good thing that ★ *God comforts us when we're discouraged*. Because if even Bible heroes can get discouraged enough to run away, imagine what can happen to us. But I'm not worried, because we're about to see how God reaches out in love to take care of us when all we can think about is running away.

BIBLE EXPLORATION

Elijah the Running Man (1 Kings 19)

Say: **On Mount Carmel, the prophet Elijah scored a huge victory for God. He challenged hundreds of false prophets to a contest. They would pray for their false gods to send fire to burn up their sacrifice. Then Elijah would pray for the true God of Israel to send fire to burn up his sacrifice.**

Elijah won that challenge. God sent down fire that burned up not only the meat of the sacrifice, but the stones of the altar, and all the water Elijah had poured over the whole thing.

Now, you would think that Elijah would be jumping with

Prep Box

Be prepared to tell about a time when you ran away as a child or thought about it, or how someone helped you get through a problem you wanted to run from.

Prep Box

Make a copy of the "Elijah's Story Quotes" handout (p. 143), cut the sections apart, and tuck them into this guide. Borrow a toaster oven from your church kitchen or bring one from home. When you arrive, start baking refrigerated biscuits or crescent rolls so kids will enjoy the aroma before they get a taste during the story. If you prefer, prebake biscuits and bring them to class.

All Together Now

joy over this great victory, but just the opposite was true. You see, he got a message from evil Queen Jezebel, who was angry that all her false prophets had been killed.

Ask a willing child to read Queen Jezebel's note.

Jezebel's Note

To the Prophet Elijah:

My husband the king told me about everything that happened on Mount Carmel today. If you think you and your God won, *you're wrong!* By this time tomorrow, you'll be as dead as my prophets. Nobody messes with me!

Jezebel, Queen of Israel

Say: **Jezebel was a queen who worshipped idols. Elijah, on the other hand, was one of God's great prophets. In fact, he was one of the greatest prophets in the whole Bible.**

So put yourself in Elijah's shoes.

Ask:

• **Describe what you think about Queen Jezebel's note.**

Say: **This is where our Bible passage takes a surprising turn. When Elijah heard the message from Queen Jezebel, he was suddenly scared to death. He forgot all about the great victory God had helped him win. He forgot that he served the God who made the universe and all that's in it. All he could think was:** *The queen is after me; the queen is after me!*

Elijah got so upset that he took off running. And Elijah was some expert runner, let me tell you.

Start running in place while I tell you the next part of the passage. And run pretty hard, because you're going to be covering some ground!

When all the kids are running in place, proceed with the passage.

Elijah ran all the way to the south end of the country. He ran like a streak, like a flash, as far away as he could go. He left his servant behind and ran on into the wilderness until he saw a broom tree. There he stopped and dropped, completely worn out.

Stop and drop!

Hand kids a broom and say: **Here's your broom tree. Rest underneath its shade.**

Elijah sat under the broom tree and prayed.

Ask:
- **What do you think Elijah said to God under that tree?**

Have a willing child read the prayer.

Elijah's Prayer

Lord, take my life. I've had enough.

Then Elijah fell into a deep sleep.

We're not sure how long Elijah slept before an angel touched him and said, "Get up and eat." Elijah looked around and there beside the broom tree sat a jug of water and some bread that had been freshly baked over warm coals.

Put half the freshly baked biscuits on a paper towel. Break up the biscuits among the children, saying with a smile: **I'm the closest thing we have to an angel this morning. Please, eat.**

Elijah drained the jug of water, ate up the tasty bread, then fell right back to sleep. Don't let your broom tree fall over while you sleep!

Later the angel woke him again. "Get up and eat, or the journey ahead will be too much for you."

Serve the remaining biscuits to the children.

Say: **Elijah ate and drank again and then continued his journey.**

Everybody get up and run in place again.

Elijah ran for 40 more days and nights until he came to the very mountain where God had given Moses the Ten Commandments. He found a cave in the mountain and went in there to spend the night.

Point to a corner of your room and say: **Pile into the cave, everyone!**

Allow time, and then say: **You'll hardly believe what happened next. God spoke to Elijah in the cave! God asked, "What are you doing here, Elijah?"**

Ask a willing child to read Elijah's answer.

Elijah Says

I've lived my whole life for you, but the Israelites have broken their promises to you, torn down your altars, and killed all your prophets. I'm the only one left, and now they're trying to kill me, too!

Say: **Poor Elijah!**

Ask:

• **What does this prayer tell you about how Elijah felt?**

Say: **But God had been watching over Elijah the entire time and was just waiting to comfort him. Isn't it good to know that ★ God comforts us when we're discouraged?**

Ask:

• **How do you know that God has been watching over Elijah so far?**

Say: **God told Elijah to go out of the cave and stand before him on the mountain.**

Everybody out of the cave! Be ready to act out what happened next. I'll read the words right from 1 Kings in the Bible.

Pause after each of the boldface words for kids to create special effects.

> And as Elijah stood there, the Lord passed by, and **a mighty windstorm** hit the mountain. It was such a terrible blast that the rocks were torn loose, but the Lord was not in the wind. After the wind there was an **earthquake,** but the Lord was not in the earthquake. And after the earthquake there was a **fire,** but the Lord was not in the fire. And after the fire there was the sound of a **gentle whisper.** When Elijah heard it, he wrapped his face in his cloak and went out and stood at the entrance of the cave. And a voice said, "What are you doing here, Elijah?"
> —1 Kings 19:11-13

Say: **Elijah repeated exactly what he'd said before.**

Point to the child who read "Elijah Says," and have that child read it again.

Say: **Then God gave Elijah directions and some *very* comforting news.**

God told Elijah to go back the way he came. On his way, he would anoint another man to be his prophet-in-training. They'd be prophets together.

So Elijah was going to have an important new friend, one who would be with him all the time.

Wave both hands at me if you think that's good news! Wave your hands, too.

But wait—that's not all!

God told Elijah that there were 7,000 people in Israel who still followed God. It turns out that Elijah wasn't as alone as he thought he was.

God comforted Elijah just as ★ *God comforts us when we're discouraged!*

Ask:

• Describe whether you would be comforted by God's instructions.

LIFE APPLICATION
. . . .

Packets of Comfort

Say: **Elijah ran a long distance—about 200 miles—before he was finally ready to listen to God at Mount Sinai. We don't have to run so far to hear from God. We have God's Word that speaks to us today, almost like a letter written directly to us. We can turn to God's Word anytime we feel discouraged.**

Look at this cool packet you get to make today! Do you know what you'll find inside? Words of God, words of comfort that you can read anytime. You don't have to run 200 miles or sleep under a broom tree or crawl into a cave. Because ★ *God comforts us when we're discouraged*, you can keep these encouraging words from the Bible with you in your pocket or backpack or purse or by your bedside!

Distribute the handouts. Before kids begin assembling, have them take turns reading the Bible verses aloud.

Ask:

• **Tell which are your favorite verses on the page, and why.**

Help kids assemble their packets according to the directions on the handouts. As they work, ask:

• **How might you share your Packets of Comfort with someone else?**

As kids finish their projects, have them clean up the craft area and join you in a circle for discussion.

All Together Now

Elijah's Story Quotes

JEZEBEL'S NOTE

To the Prophet Elijah:
My husband the king told me about everything that happened on Mount Carmel today. If you think you and your God won, you're wrong! By this time tomorrow, you'll be as dead as my prophets.
Nobody messes with me!

Jezebel

QUEEN OF ISRAEL

ELIJAH SAYS

I've lived my whole life for you, but the Israelites have broken their promises to you, torn down your altars, and killed all your prophets. I'm the only one left, and now they're trying to kill me, too!

ELIJAH'S PRAYER

Lord, take my life. I've had enough.

Published in *All Together Now, Volume 4* by Group Publishing, Inc., 1515 Cascade Ave., Loveland, CO 80538.

143

Packet of Comfort

Cut out both pieces below. Line them up back to back with the dots on the left, and glue the two strips together. Fold the right edges to the center. Punch the dots with a paper punch. Run a length of raffia through the holes. Then fold those edges to the center. Wrap the raffia around the packet and tie.

YOU WILL KEEP IN PERFECT PEACE ALL WHO TRUST IN YOU, ALL WHOSE THOUGHTS ARE FIXED ON YOU!
ISAIAH 26:3

YOUR HEAVENLY FATHER ALREADY KNOWS ALL YOUR NEEDS. SEEK THE KINGDOM OF GOD ABOVE ALL ELSE, AND LIVE RIGHTEOUSLY, AND HE WILL GIVE YOU EVERYTHING YOU NEED.
MATTHEW 6:32-33

THE EYES OF THE LORD WATCH OVER THOSE WHO DO RIGHT; HIS EARS ARE OPEN TO THEIR CRIES FOR HELP. THE LORD HEARS HIS PEOPLE WHEN THEY CALL TO HIM FOR HELP. HE RESCUES THEM FROM ALL THEIR TROUBLES.
PSALM 34:15, 17

DON'T WORRY ABOUT ANYTHING; INSTEAD, PRAY ABOUT EVERYTHING. TELL GOD WHAT YOU NEED, AND THANK HIM FOR ALL HE HAS DONE. THEN YOU WILL EXPERIENCE GOD'S PEACE... HIS PEACE WILL GUARD YOUR HEARTS AND MINDS AS YOU LIVE IN CHRIST JESUS.
PHILIPPIANS 4:6-7

GIVE YOUR BURDENS TO THE LORD, AND HE WILL TAKE CARE OF YOU. HE WILL NOT PERMIT THE GODLY TO SLIP AND FALL.
PSALM 55:22

AND WE KNOW THAT GOD CAUSES EVERYTHING TO WORK TOGETHER FOR THE GOOD OF THOSE WHO LOVE GOD AND ARE CALLED ACCORDING TO HIS PURPOSE FOR THEM.
ROMANS 8:28

COMMITMENT

. . . .

Listening for God

Say: **There was a lot of rowdy action in our Bible passage, so I'm wondering if you caught one important detail that makes a whole lot of difference in our lives today.**

Ask:

• *How* **did God speak to Elijah?**

Say: **God didn't speak in the howling wind or the earthquake or the fire—but in a whispering voice.**

Ask:

• **How do you think God speaks to us today?**

Say: **God speaks to us when we're listening for him. When we're listening for God, we're quiet. We're not praying for big lists of things, we're just quiet.**

Ask:

• **Describe what you think it means to be truly quiet before God.**

• **What's a good time and place for you to be quiet before God?**

Say: ★ *God comforts us when we're discouraged* **if we give him time to speak to us. God isn't going to bombard our day with flights of angels or fireworks or great thundering voices from heaven. God speaks to us in the quiet, just as he spoke to Elijah.**

CLOSING

. . . .

Prayer for Quiet

Say: **Finding moments of quiet can be difficult. It means turning everything off, tuning everything out, and focusing all our thoughts on God, who made us, loves us, and is just waiting for us to give him our attention. Let's close by asking God to help us find quiet moments this week.**

Pray: **Dear God, thank you that you're always there, waiting to** ★ *comfort us when we're discouraged.* **We pray that you'll help us find quiet moments with you this week. Thank you for hearing our prayers. In Jesus' name, amen.**

The Amazing Discovery of King Josiah

LESSON AIM

To help kids know that ★ *you're never too young to make a difference for God.*

OBJECTIVES

Kids will

- ✓ play Quick, You're King/Queen,
- ✓ experience what young King Josiah did with his marvelous discovery,
- ✓ explore ways they can make a difference, and
- ✓ pledge to be difference-makers.

BIBLE BASIS

 2 Kings 22:1–23:30; 2 Chronicles 34:1–35:24

"Josiah was eight years old when he became king" (2 Kings 22:1). Who takes care of an 8-year-old king? Does the young boy carry any royal decision-making power? Who are the influencers in his life? What's the balance of power among them?

We know this about Josiah's family: His grandfather Manasseh did all the evil things as king of Judah that Ahab had done as king of Israel. Manasseh filled the streets of Jerusalem with the blood of innocent people, led God's people into idol worship, and did everything he could to destroy the worship of the one true God. Manasseh's true delight seemed to be in irritating God. In judgment, God promised to bring such disaster on

You'll need...

- ☐ small paper or plastic cup for each child (empty, clean yogurt cups work well, too)
- ☐ CD or MP3 player with lively music
- ☐ silver jewelry or faux silver beads in a small box
- ☐ small Bible
- ☐ sledgehammer
- ☐ 4 copies of the "Road Rally Banner" (p. 152)
- ☐ small treat, such as a plate of strawberries*
- ☐ copies of the "Make a Pack o' Difference" handout (p. 156)
- ☐ scissors
- ☐ glue sticks

* Always check for allergies before serving snacks.

Israel and Judah that the ears of everyone who heard about it would tingle (2 Kings 21:12). This awful king reigned 55 years.

Josiah's father continued in Manasseh's ways. He reigned only two years before his own courtiers killed him, bringing Josiah to the throne at age 8 with anything but a stellar heritage.

But Josiah was not to be tainted by the sins of his fathers. Among his godly influencers would have been the high priest Hilkiah and his son, the prophet Jeremiah. There was Shaphan, the royal scribe, as well as Shallum, the keeper of the wardrobe whose wife was the prophetess Huldah.

The Chronicles account tells us that Josiah began to seek the God of his father David when he was 16. At the age of 20 or 26, depending on whether you follow the timeline of Chronicles or Kings, with the reigns of control firmly in his hands, he initiated major repairs to the long-neglected Temple. The repair work uncovered a hidden scroll of the Law. It was Josiah's response to what he heard in the book of the Law that endeared the young king to God's heart and set back Jerusalem's destruction for a few years.

Josiah tore his clothes like a man in mourning. He had just heard the judgments that God would pass on his people if they deserted his way. Josiah sent a delegation to inquire of the prophetess Huldah what should be done. Huldah explained that God was pleased with Josiah's repentance.

Josiah stood in front of the Temple, read the Law to the people, and reaffirmed their covenant with God. Then he cleared all remnants of idol worship from the Temple and set out to destroy every pagan temple and altar in the land. That spring, Josiah led Israel and Judah in their first Passover feast since the time of Samuel. It was a time of great renewal and rejoicing in the land.

Unfortunately Josiah's life came to an early end at age 39 as he led his army to an impossible battle against King Neco of Egypt who marched through Judah and Israel to meet up with the armies of Assyria. Josiah received a mortal wound in the battle. He was brought by chariot back to Jerusalem and there he died. The young, charismatic king who'd done so much good was greatly mourned by his people. Scripture closes the life of Josiah with this resounding epitaph:

Never before had there been a king like Josiah, who turned to the Lord with all his heart and soul and strength, obeying all the laws of Moses. And there has never been a king like him since.
—2 Kings 23:25

All Together Now

1 Timothy 4:12

"Don't let anyone think less of you because you are young. Be an example to all believers in what you say, in the way you live, in your love, your faith, and your purity."

The Apostle Paul wrote these words to his young companion, Timothy. We can't be sure of Timothy's age when he encountered Paul. Some suggest that he may have been in his teens, though these are just guesses.

Timothy was born of a Jewish mother and Greek father, but was raised by his devout mother and grandmother. He was already a Christian when he met Paul.

Rabbinic teaching emphasized the importance of respecting elders, especially educated elders. It's easy to see why a young, half-Greek lad might encounter some difficulty receiving the respect Paul felt he innately deserved. Because Timothy was neither fully Jew nor fully Greek, he would probably have been an outcast in both societies. But Paul saw in his young companion a spiritual maturity that naturally cast Timothy in leadership roles and demanded that churches under his purview recognize Timothy in this way also. Early Christians might argue with Timothy because of his youth, but they would accept Paul's judgment.

There are Timothys among us. We can recognize them by their urgent passion for God and maturity beyond their years. I'm fortunate to be part of a congregation that brings in bright young interns each year. Some of them turn out to be too outstanding to let go.

Not all those with hearts for God like Josiah and Timothy are born to privilege or find advocates like Paul. Who will help them? Take a peek in your mirror.

UNDERSTANDING YOUR KIDS

Some kids seem to appear in our lives with hearts already finely tuned toward God. This is a precious way God has gifted some kids. Josiah may have been just such a child. As was David. We can be on the lookout for spiritually gifted children and give them the sensitive spiritual guidance they need.

Other children also become aware of God's love for them and his call on their lives as they pass through the Sunday school years. These are crucial years for spiritual development when young hearts are open to God's tender call for their commitment.

Kids from homes where parents take an active role in their kids' faith development may come to you as bulwarks of Bible knowledge.

Don't worry—you still have an eminently important role to play in their lives. Your teaching makes biblical events jump off the page and take hold in the lives of these children as never before.

No matter what the stage of their faith development, kids often feel frustrated by the limitations of being young. If only they could go out on their own. If only they could drive. The "if onlys" go on and on. Learning things that can make a difference in God's kingdom and then taking small steps that *do* make a difference brings a remarkable sense of empowerment to kids. Use this lesson to teach kids that ★ *you're never too young to make a difference for God.*

All Together Now

ATTENTION GRABBER

Quick, You're King/Queen!

Give kids a warm welcome and tell them to prepare for a game that's full of surprises.

Distribute cups and have kids practice balancing the cups on their heads. Next, have them move around, still balancing their cups.

Say: **That's how we're going to play our game. It's called Quick, You're King! or Quick, You're Queen! Form a big circle. When I start the music, you'll start doing fun, silly motions to the music. When the cup falls off your head, drop to the ground. The last one standing is King or Queen of our group for 10 seconds. In that 10 seconds, the King or Queen gives a royal decree of one truly good thing he or she would do as ruler to make a difference for everyone in our group.**

Explain that Kings and Queens need to come up with new ideas each time. Once Kings and Queens have "ruled" and given a royal decree, they drop out of the circle and cheer for the rest of the kids.

Start the music. Stop the music as soon as you have a winner. Keep playing rounds of the game until each child has had an opportunity to rule. Then gather kids in a discussion circle, and ask:

• **How did it feel to "rule" for 10 seconds?**

• **Which ideas did you feel would truly make a difference in everyone's lives—and why?**

• **What was fun about ruling? What was hard about it?**

Say: **Our Bible passage today is about a child who became king in Judah when he was only 8 years old. Eight years old! And guess what—along the way we'll learn that ★*you're never too young to make a difference for God.***

Prep Box

Set up a CD or MP3 music player with lively music. You'll also need a small paper or plastic cup for each child.

BIBLE EXPLORATION

The Amazing Discovery of King Josiah

(2 Kings 22:1–23:30; 2 Chronicles 34:1–35:24)

Ask:

• **What would be good about becoming king if you were 8 years old?**

• **What might be hard about it?**

Say: **Our young king's name is Josiah. His grandfather had been a terrible king who tried to get rid of everyone who loved God. Josiah's grandfather set up places to worship false gods everywhere. That terrible king ruled a long time. Then Josiah's father ruled only two years. He didn't love God either.**

But when young Josiah became king, the people who took care of him and taught him had strong hopes that this young man would be different. We're going to go on a road trip—called a Road Rally—to find out why.

I've hidden the directions for our first rally point somewhere in this room. I wonder who will find it.

When the children find the Rally Banner, lead them to the door of your room. Ask them to choose a Captain for this leg of your journey. Remind them that while you're having lots of fun, other people in the church are meeting, so you need to have a quiet road rally. Then give the Rally Banner to the Captain, and have the Captain lead kids to the first discovery.

Gather the children around the box of silver, and say: **When King Josiah was about 16, he saw that God's Temple needed to be repaired. It used to be a magnificent building shining in Jerusalem, calling people to worship God. But it had been neglected for years upon years. Josiah wanted God's house to shine like it used to. So he ordered it to be repaired. While the workers began to repair the Temple, somehow they stumbled upon a long-lost secret. We'll find out about that secret at our next rally point.**

Take the box of silver, have kids choose a new Captain, and follow the Captain to the next rally point where you'll find a small Bible.

Say: **The long-lost secret the Temple workers found was the book of God's laws. Someone had cleverly hidden this copy in the Temple—we don't know exactly where. Hilkiah, the high priest, found this book. He told Shaphan, who was Josiah's court secretary. Shaphan read it to King Josiah.**

The king realized how badly the people had broken God's law. He tore his robes in two and cried in sorrow. He sent his closest advisers to a prophetess to ask what to do. She said that God saw how sorry King Josiah was for all the sins of the people. God knew about Josiah's faithful heart and loved him.

Prep Box

Plan where you'll hide the three items kids will find on the Road Rally: the small box with silver jewelry or faux silver beads, the small Bible, and the sledgehammer. Write the directions to the box of silver on the back of a Rally Banner that you'll hide in your meeting area. For instance, you might write, "Turn left down the hall, go up the stairs, and look behind the large plant." Hide the box of silver there and with it leave a Rally Banner with directions to the small Bible. Hide the Bible and with it leave a Rally Banner with directions to the sledgehammer. Hide the sledgehammer and with it leave a Rally Banner with directions to return to the meeting area. If the weather is nice, you may want to place some of your items outside. Also, hide a small treat, such as a plate of strawberries, in your room.

Even though Josiah was still a teenager, he got right to work. Let's get to our next checkpoint to find out what he did.

Take the Bible. Have kids choose a new Captain and find their way to the next checkpoint where they'll find a sledgehammer.

Say: **Whoa!**

Ask:

• **What is something like this used for?**

Say: **And that's exactly what King Josiah used it for. He got busy knocking down all the idols set up by his grandfather. They were everywhere—in the Temple, in high places all around the country, inside city gates, by special altars. Josiah worked hard to make sure not a single one was left standing.**

He let everyone know that the people of Judah and Israel would serve the one true God and the one true God only.

Show the Bible.

King Josiah stood by one of the pillars of the Temple and read the laws to the people. He renewed the promises between God and the people—the promises made so long ago by Abraham.

And then he did something that brought great delight to everyone.

Pick up the sledgehammer. Have the children choose a new Captain to guide them back to the room where you've hidden a small treat.

When you've returned to the room, say: **By the time King Josiah was done with all his work, he was probably about 26 years old—still a young king. He ordered all the people to come to Jerusalem and celebrate the Passover feast like it used to be celebrated. And what a celebration it was! They did everything just like the book of the law told them, and everyone rejoiced in God.**

The people of Judah loved their king and learned that ★ *you're never too young to make a difference for God.*

Now, I didn't prepare a whole Passover feast for you, but I thought that because we've discovered ★ *you're never too young to make a difference for God,* **we should have a small celebration.**

Hand out your strawberries or other small treat.

Ask:

• **What is your favorite part of King Josiah's life—and why?**

All Together Now

• How does King Josiah's life make you think differently about being young?

LIFE APPLICATION

Make a Difference

Say: **People loved King Josiah because he made a difference for God even though he was young. You may not be kings and queens, but you can still make a mighty big difference for God right where you live. The ideas on this handout will show you that ★** *you're never too young to make a difference for God.*

Invite a willing child to read the "difference-maker" strips on the handouts.

Ask:

• **How could doing each of these things make a difference for God?**

• **Describe whether you think small things like these** *really* **make a difference.**

• **Has anyone ever done something like this for you? What kind of difference did it make in your life?**

Lead kids through the simple assembly instructions detailed on the handout.

Prep Box

Prepare a finished "Make a Pack o' Difference" project for kids to see and examine. In your craft area, set out copies of the "Make a Pack o' Difference" handout (p. 156), scissors, and glue sticks.

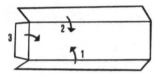

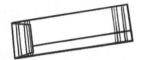

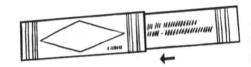

COMMITMENT

Difference-Makers

Gather kids in a circle with their completed Pack o' Difference projects.

Ask:

• **Which of these projects do you think you'll do first? Why those?**

• **What do you think might happen when you do those projects?**

• **Which projects might be more difficult for you? Explain.**

• **Why might they be worth doing even though they're more difficult?**

Have kids talk to a partner about their plans for tackling their Pack o' Difference projects. Encourage partners to tell each other

Make a Pack o' Difference

Can you make a difference for God's kingdom? You bet you can! And here are some simple ways to get you started.

Make your Pack o' Difference by cutting out the large pack below. Turn it over to the blank side, and fold in on all the fold lines.

Run a strip of glue where the back edges cross. Press them down a minute until they are well stuck.

Then run a strip of glue across the bottom piece. Fold it up and hold it in place until it's stuck as well. Now your packet is ready for gum...er...I mean difference-makers!

Cut apart the six difference-makers to the right. Carefully slide them into the packet.

Now go be a difference-maker for God's kingdom!

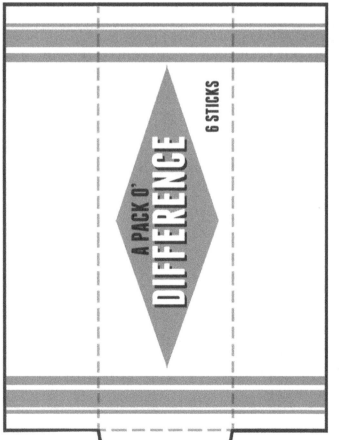

A PACK O' DIFFERENCE

6 STICKS

BE COOPERATIVE WITH MOM OR DAD, EVEN WHEN YOU DON'T FEEL LIKE IT.

ASK A PARENT TO HELP YOU TAKE FLOWERS TO SOMEONE WHO DOESN'T GET OUT MUCH.

MAKE A FUN NOTE OF ENCOURAGEMENT FOR SOMEONE WHO NEEDS IT.

BE FRIENDLY TO SOMEONE WHO ISN'T FRIENDLY TO YOU.

DO AN EXTRA CHORE IN SECRET — MORE THAN ONCE!

GIVE A FOOT RUB TO A TIRED PARENT.

when they'll begin and who they'll surprise. After a couple of minutes, have partners report back to the large group, with kids telling their partners' plans.

Ask:

• **Suppose you thought of other difference-making projects and kept up with ideas like this for an entire year. How would your life and the lives of the people you touch be different?**

Say: **If you think being a difference-maker is worth it, stand up.** Pause. **That's terrific! Because I know this for sure:** ★ *You're never too young to make a difference for God.* **If you ask him, God will show you all kinds of ways to be a difference-maker. Perhaps you will want to write them down on extra strips of paper and add them to your packet.**

CLOSING

. . . .

Affirmation

Say: **Before you leave today, give high fives to everyone in the room and say,** ★ *"You're never too young to make a difference for God!"*

Kids' Travel Guide™ Series

Kids' Travel Guide to the Armor of God

The world is a scary place, but God is greater than it all! This edition of the *Kids' Travel Guide* series leads your Sunday school or midweek program on a 13-week Scripture-based exploration of the armor of God. Lead them to have a faith so bold they'll be able to stand firm in the midst of terrifying or unclear situations. Kids (levels K-5th grade) will explore how to be strong in the decisions they make, and in relationships with others. *Kids' Travel Guide™ to the Armor of God* is perfect for helping children learn about spiritual issues in a non-threatening and empowering way. **Flexible**—works for 2 kids…12 kids…20 kids!

▶ ISBN 978-0-7644-2695-7 • $19.99

Kids' Travel Guide to the 23rd Psalm
▶ ISBN 978-0-7644-4005-2
$19.99

Kids' Travel Guide to the Fruit of the Spirit
▶ ISBN 978-0-7644-2390-1
$19.99

Kids' Travel Guide to the Lord's Prayer
▶ ISBN 978-0-7644-2524-0
$19.99

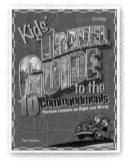

Kids' Travel Guide to the Ten Commandments
▶ ISBN 978-0-7644-2224-9
$19.99

Each book includes 13 lessons with these fun features to help take your kids on a travel adventure:

- **In-Focus Verse** around which the adventure is focused.
- **Departure Prayer** designed for children to add their own words of prayer.
- **First-Stop Discoveries:** Narrated enactment or group activity exploring the lesson's Bible story.
- **Story Excursions:** Through Bible stories, bring the book's biblical theme to life in fun, imaginative, and dramatic ways.
- **Adventures in Growing:** Activities show kids how to apply what they've learned to their daily lives!
- **Souvenirs:** Kids create pages that go into a notebook (their very own travel journal!) to remind them of the lesson's Bible point.

Secret weapons for *getting kids' attention!*

Throw & Tell® Balls

Group's Throw & Tell Balls get—and keep—kids' attention when you finish a lesson early, kids show up grumpy, or you need an icebreaker—fast! Simply inflate a sturdy, colorful ball and let kids toss the ball around for a few seconds. When you call "Time," the child holding the ball reads what's written under his or her left thumb—and then everyone answers (or the child answers, depending on how you choose to play). Kids love the Throw & Tell Balls, and you'll love seeing them open up, laugh, and connect with one another in this new way.

NOTE: *All balls inflate to 24" diameter. Comes in hangable bag.*

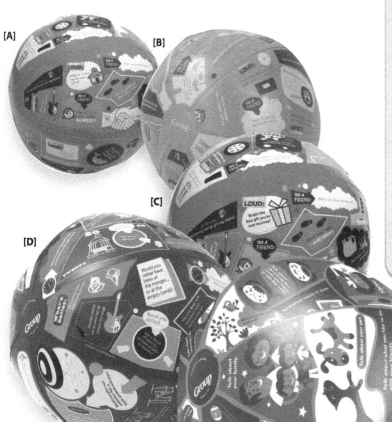

[A]
[B]
[C]
[D]
[E]
[F]

THROW & TELL BALLS *For age 3+ only*

[A] ATTENTION-GRABBER THROW & TELL BALL *for Children's Ministry*
Perfect for grabbing kids' attention, then launching your lessons!
▶ UPC 646847-10995-9 • $9.99 *In Canada $10.99*

[B] PRAYER THROW & TELL BALL *for Children's Ministry*
53 prayer prompts help kids learn more about poverty.
▶ UPC 646847-12156-2 • $9.99 *In Canada $10.99*

[C] ALL ABOUT ME THROW & TELL BALL *for Children's Ministry*
Encourage kids to learn about each other and find common connections!
▶ UPC 646847-16933-5 • $9.99 *In Canada $10.99*

[D] THIS...OR THAT? THROW & TELL BALL *for Preteen Ministry*
Keep kids on the edge of their seats with this hilarious ball of fully loaded questions.
▶ UPC 646847-16934-2 • $9.99 *In Canada $10.99*

[E] PRESCHOOL THROW & TELL BALL *for Preschool Ministry*
It's fun. It's super-easy. It's bouncy. And it's GUARANTEED to get your preschoolers to open up and interact!
▶ ISBN 978-0-7644-7613-6 • $9.99 *In Canada $10.99*

[F] LIFE-APPLICATION THROW & TELL BALL *for Children's Ministry*
Dozens of instant application activities!
▶ UPC 646847-10988-1 • $9.99 *In Canada $10.99*

> I teach our 3rd - 5th grade Sunday school class and also our pre-k second hour class. I used this for both classes and the kids had a blast answering the questions about themselves and learning about their friends.
>
> —*Children's Ministry Leader, Lawton, OK*

Order today! Visit group.com or your favorite Christian retailer.